D0209814

A
WILLIAM MAXWELL
PORTRAIT

Books by William Maxwell

NOVELS
Bright Center of Heaven (1934)
They Came Like Swallows (1937)
The Folded Leaf (1945)
Time Will Darken It (1948)
The Château (1961)
So Long, See You Tomorrow (1980)

STORIES
Over By the River and Other Stories (1977)
Billie Dyer and Other Stories (1992)
All the Days and Nights: Collected Stories (1994)

MEMOIR
Ancestors: A Family History (1971)

ESSAYS
The Outermost Dream: Essays and Reviews (1989)

TALES
The Old Man at the Railroad Crossing (1966)

CHILDREN'S STORIES
The Heavenly Tenants (1946)
Mrs. Donald's Dog Bun and His Home Away from Home (1995)

LETTERS
The Happiness of Getting It Down Right:
Letters of Frank O'Connor and William Maxwell
edited by Michael Steinman (1996)

The Element of Lavishness: Letters of Sylvia Townsend
Warner and William Maxwell, 1938–1978
edited by Michael Steinman (2001)

A
WILLIAM MAXWELL
PORTRAIT

Memories and Appreciations

EDITED BY

Charles Baxter, Michael Collier,

and Edward Hirsch

W. W. Norton & Company
New York   London

The frontispiece photograph of William Maxwell is reprinted with the kind permission of the photographer, Sara Barrett.

Because this page cannot legibly accommodate all the copyright notices, pages 233–34 constitute an extension of the copyright page.

For information about permission to reproduce selections from this book, write to Permissions, W. W. Norton & Company, Inc., 500 Fifth Avenue, New York, NY 10110

Manufacturing by Quebecor Fairfield
Book design by Brooke Koven
Production manager: Julia Druskin

Library of Congress Cataloging-in-Publication Data

A William Maxwell portrait : memories and appreciations / edited by Charles Baxter, Michael Collier, and Edward Hirsch.— 1st ed.
    p. cm.
ISBN 0-393-05771-2
  1. Maxwell, William, 1908– 2. Maxwell, William, 1908– —Friends and associates. 3. Authors, American—20th century—Biography. 4. Authors and publishers—United States. 5. Literature publishing—United States. 6. Editors—United States—Biography. 7. New Yorker (New York, N.Y. : 1925) I. Baxter, Charles, date. II. Collier, Michael, date. III. Hirsch, Edward.
PS3525.A9464Z97 2004
813'.54—dc22

                                        2004009730

W. W. Norton & Company, Inc.
500 Fifth Avenue, New York, N.Y. 10110
www.wwnorton.com

W. W. Norton & Company Ltd.
Castle House, 75/76 Wells Street, London W1T 3QT

1 2 3 4 5 6 7 8 9 0

Contents

Acknowledgments

THE EDITORS would like to express gratitude to those writers who contributed essays to this volume. We are particularly grateful for Alec Wilkinson's many helpful suggestions, for Michael Steinman's guidance, and for Kate and Brookie Maxwell's support. Thanks to Ellen Bryant Voigt for early conversations at the Bread Loaf Writers' Conference, where the idea for *A William Maxwell Portrait* took shape. Finally, unending admiration for our editor, Carol Houck Smith, whose love and appreciation of the work and life of William Maxwell is expressed by her commitment to this book and by the many hours she spent helping us bring it to completion.

Introduction

THE STORIES THAT writers like to tell about other writers often are accounts of amusing or slightly sinister wrongdoing. Stories, after all, begin when things start to go wrong. We tend to love troublemakers in fiction but would be horrified if they came into our lives; even the arrival of their authors might be cause for alarm. Rascals are usually best kept at a distance. Sometimes, when misbehavior graduates to monstrosity or simple self-destructiveness, the anecdotes that writers tell about other writers stop being funny, but even then they perpetuate the myth of the artist as public clown and domestic criminal, the half-mad rogue romantic prophet whose self-centered manias have stoked the fires that burn within the work.

How can great art be created by loathsome human beings? History has proven conclusively that it can be, and by now only Puritans and the simple-minded still believe that an exemplary life is a requirement for the production of exemplary art. The Republic of Arts and Letters is peopled by every sort of character, and goodness, as it happens, is not a requirement for entry there. The perfectly chosen adjective may get you in, and committing a murder will not keep you out. Gesualdo, Caravaggio, Ben Jonson.

By contrast, goodness—a certain variety of it—what John Updike in these pages calls "excellence" and Alice Munro calls "honour," in the life and work of William Maxwell, has called forth this collection of tributes, and what all these memories and appreciations have in common is a kind of astonishment. Maxwell was a very rare human being; there seems to have been almost no one like him in his own time in American letters, perhaps ever. There was something so unusual in his example and in his work that we have all—the editors and contributors to this volume—struggled to say what that *something* was, but whatever this quality may have been, it had nothing to do with the myth of the artist as romantic destructive egotist. Instead, the opposite: his work often contains passions of every sort, and he himself was noted, time and again, for his generosity, and not just as an editor or as a friend or mentor. He inspired, at least in some of us, a kind of wonderment: where did he come from, how did he get this way, and what elements went into these beautiful books that he gave to the world?

An inventory of possible nouns—generosity, loyalty, artistry—will not do. We are dealing with life and work so remarkable that some testimony is required. Those who love his books or may have only a passing acquaintance with them will find these tributes adding up to a collective portrait of one of the finest writers of our time.

MAXWELL WAS BORN in Lincoln, Illinois, in 1908 and died in 2000, in New York City. During his life he published six novels, three collections of stories, a memoir, a volume of literary essays and reviews, a collection of letters, a collection of tales, and two children's books. From 1936 to 1976 he was an editor at *The New Yorker*, where he worked with authors such as Eudora Welty, John Hersey, Vladimir Nabokov, John Updike, John Cheever, Larry Woiwode, and many others. His honors include the American Book Award for *So Long, See You Tomorrow*, the PEN/Malamud Award, the Gold Medal for Fiction from the American Academy of Arts and Letters, and the Ivan Sandrof Award for Distinguished Service to American Letters from the National Book Critics Circle. Maxwell was educated at the University of Illinois and spent a year at Harvard as a graduate student, where he made a lifelong friend of Robert Fitzgerald. From the mid-thirties until his death he lived almost continuously in New York City, where he married Emily Noyes and raised two daughters, Kate and Brookie.

—THE EDITORS

A
WILLIAM MAXWELL
PORTRAIT

John Updike

Stolen

Please go on being yourself.
—From my last letter from
William Maxwell, July 28, 2000

What is it like, to be a stolen painting—
to be Rembrandt's "Storm on the Sea of Galilee"
or "The Concert," by Vermeer, both burglarized,
along with "Chez Tortoni" by Manet,
and some Degases, from the Isabella Stewart
Gardner Museum, in Boston, twelve years ago?

Think of how bored they get, stacked
in the warehouse somewhere, say in Mattapan,
gazing at the back of the butcher paper
they are wrapped in, instead of at
the rapt glad faces of those who love art.

Only criminals know where they are.
The gloom of criminality enshrouds them.

Why have we been stolen? they ask themselves.
Who has benefitted? Or do they hang
admired in some sheikh's sandy palace,
or the vault of a mad Manila tycoon?

In their captivity, they may dream of rescue
but cannot cry for help. Their paint
is inert and crackled, their linen friable.
They have one stratagem, the same old one:
to be themselves, on and on.

The boat tilts frozen on the storm's wild wave.
The concert has halted between two notes.
An interregnum, sufficiently extended,
becomes an absence. When wise
and kindly men die, who will restore
disappeared excellence to its throne?

Donna Tartt

Mr. Maxwell

I REMEMBER very well the first time I ever heard William Maxwell's name. I had just written my first novel, and I was in the offices of Alfred A. Knopf, having just finished my first extensive press interview. I had ventured into the interview with a youngster's anticipatory flush—all eagerness to please—and emerged from it so harrowed that I had made a special trip up to the Knopf offices to tell them that, in the future, I thought I should do things differently. If reporters submitted to me their questions, on paper, I would then give them typed answers—more considered and literate answers than they would otherwise receive. After all, I was a writer; I expressed myself best on the page and not when prodded to talk into a tape recorder. It was a horror to have my agitated responses to intrusive questions chopped up and re-arranged and presented in print as if they were the worthy equal of my written words. Surely they could understand. But as I struggled to make my point, I became aware that the two men to whom I was speaking (publicist, editor, old hands at the game, both of them) were looking at each other in a highly amused fashion.

"You can't do that, kid," said the publicist. "No way. Forget it."

The editor—it was his job, I now realize, to play Good Cop to the publicist's Bad Cop—shrugged whimsically and said: "I'm sorry, sweetie."

"But why not?" I said.

"Because nobody does it," said the publicist, hands on hips, looking at a spot somewhere above my head. "What is this, the nineteenth century? I mean, you've *got* to do TV, you've *got* to do radio, you've *got* to reach a mass audience, that's *just the way it is, kid.* None of our authors do their interviews *in writing.*"

"Well, one author does," the editor said, tolerantly, leaning back at his desk and lighting a cigarette. "William Maxwell."

"But if he does it," I said, "then why can't I?"

"Because he's an old guy. And you're not."

And that was that. The subject was adroitly changed; I was maneuvered out of the office, and I went home on the subway, having lost the battle (there was never any chance of my winning it) and feeling a sullen sympathy with William Maxwell, whoever he was.

. . .

AS IT HAPPENED, a little less than a year later I was lucky enough to meet Mr. Maxwell, at a small dinner party given by a mutual friend. By this time I knew very well who he was: colleague of Thurber and Mitchell and E. B. White in the glory days of *The New Yorker;* legendary editor of Salinger, Welty, Nabokov, and too many other illustrious names to mention; and a distinguished essayist and novelist in his own right. I remember feeling nervous and shy, riding uptown in the taxicab, not quite sure what to expect from the evening ahead. I was used to literary lions who behaved like lions: boasting, sprawling, sulky, unpredictable in their whims and enthusiams, apt to roar (and sometimes pounce) if roused. But—as I soon discovered—Mr. Maxwell was a lion of a different and finer order: no man-eater, but an Aslan. From the moment he took my hand, it was radiantly apparent to me that I was in the presence of one of the gentlest and most charming persons I'd ever met.

Love at first sight? I can safely say that I loved him the instant I saw him. He carried himself carefully (age had made him frail) but as old as he was—well into his eighties then—he was still very handsome. His spare Midwestern elegance—all long arms and legs—was reminiscent of Fred Astaire: not the tuxedoed boulevardier of the thirties and forties but Astaire in his later incarnation, after he'd stopped dancing, when it was more than enough to see him padding around quietly in the films wearing an old cardigan sweater, being his own graceful, offhand, angelic self. Mr. Maxwell emanated a similar grace, very American, which was at once small-town and quietly urbane: one saw the New Yorker in him very clearly, but also, with equal clarity, the bashful young man from central Illinois. But by far his most endearing feature (the one that impressed me most at first meeting, the one that stays with me still) was his wide-open expression: vulnerable, receptive, with nothing about it of age or cynicism. He might have been a boy of six, to watch the thoughts passing so transparently over his face.

I remember, when I was a child in Mississippi, having a fond idea that when writers got together they talked about literature. What I envisioned, and pined for, was a community rather like the one at the end of Truffaut's *Fahrenheit 451:* where people were consumed by books, ruled and driven and utterly possessed by them, where they walked around preoccupied in the snow like monks walking the Stations of the Cross and recited *Jane Eyre* or *The Weir of Hermiston* out loud to themselves. And it was a bitter disappointment when I finally got to New York and—instead of passionate discussions of Latin poetry, or arguments about *Anna Karenina*—I found that "literary" conversations were not terribly different from the gossipy party conversations that I'd overheard at my parents' house when I was growing up.

But Mr. Maxwell struck a balance which fell pleasantly between social nicety and my fanatical ideals. For all his gentleness of manner, he was bracingly strong-minded in his reverence for literature. (Of his august elders when he was a young man at *The New Yorker*, he remarked, with his customary mildness: "Well, of course they went out every night, and saw all the latest shows. But they'd scarcely read a word of Tolstoy. And I don't call that very sophisticated, do you?") Yet even his casual conversation was illumined with the generosity, the tolerant and clear-headed sweetness that characterizes his written work. He told a story, I remember, about some minor something or other that had happened in his apartment building; the story is forgotten, but not the way he told it: light, ineffable, perfect. It was like hearing Chekhov talk.

If the problem with books—as Plato said—is that books cannot talk back, how lovely, then, to be in the same room with an intelligence as warm and responsive as Mr. Maxwell's! One wanted to pour out one's very heart to him, so that my overriding memory of the evening is of trying to restrain myself from doing just that. But—unable to contain myself—I did blurt out the story of what had happened to me at the publisher's office (the incident had preyed much on my mind) and as I spoke he leaned toward me and listened with a quite genuine sympathy and distress which reminded me of the alert and slightly alarmed way that my mother used to listen to me when I came home and told her about some outrageous injustice which had happened to me at school. I can't remember what he said to me, apart from assuring me that my instinct to stick to the written word was both serious and correct. But I remember very well the way he listened—and I remember too that he didn't laugh. I'd told the story as if it were funny (feeling that I had no other excuse for telling it) and that made me love him as much as anything—realizing that he saw through my effort to be amusing, and that he took me more seriously than I took myself.

At the end of the evening, he inscribed a copy of *So Long, See You Tomorrow* for me, thanking *me* for asking him to sign it when of course the favor was quite the other way around. I was too polite to read the inscription when he handed the book back to me across the table, but—as soon as I was alone in the cab—opened it right up (though I had to wait until we were stopped at a bright intersection before I could make the words out). I don't know what I'd expected, but certainly nothing quite this modest and soft-spoken:

> Dear Donna,
> I hope you like my farmers—
> Bill

• • •

IT WAS SAID OF Oscar Wilde—great conversationalist that he was—that the secret of his charm was his ability to focus the whole of his attention upon the person he was talking to, so that, in the concentrated glow of his company, one felt as if one was the only other person in the world. And this was also true of Mr. Maxwell. As any reader can see from his work, he was warmly interested in people—"what people said and did and wore and ate and hoped for and were afraid of." He loved biography and memoir, diaries and letters, and he relished in the humblest details of individual lives: the croquet parties of an unknown Victorian clergyman, the sweetmeats, the unexpected rainstorms, the sheepdogs in the flowerbeds; the grand piano and the "withered, spidery plants" in the crowded communal apartment of a dissident in Soviet Moscow. As for the great: from the confusing and often sensational avalanche of documentary evidence about Lord Byron's life, he unhesitatingly selects the perfect, quiet detail that brings Byron instantly to life. ("The picture of him that sticks in my mind is Thomas Moore's statement that while dining at Newstead Abbey Byron would pass a glass of wine over his shoulder to his superannuated butler, who was standing behind his chair.")

But, careful observer of human nature that he was, Mr. Maxwell was no detached spectator, drawing out others solely for his own entertainment; even with strangers, he seemed more comfortable with intimate conversation than with chit-chat, and he was equally generous with his own life, his own stories. I remember one evening in particular, at a different dinner party (a rather grand one thrown by a famous hostess and full of all sorts of exalted & noisy personages) where he and I happened to be seated together. He was certainly the oldest guest at the party; I was certainly the youngest. Around us at the table it was all shop talk, sports talk, media-magnate gossip, politics; his wife, Emily, who was the more sociable of the pair, was participating cheerfully in the conversation but Mr. Maxwell—I could well

see it by the bleak way he was staring at the centerpiece—
was no more interested in baseball or in the New York
City council race than I was. Silently we sat, side by side,
companionable in our reticence, aware of each other
but not saying a word, like two children at a table full of
grown-ups.

And as soon as the conversation had spiraled wholly
out of our orbit, he turned unhesitatingly to me. Was I a
night owl? he inquired, in his quiet, confidential voice,
so that I had to lean close to hear him. It was rather late
for him—he was old, and even though he didn't sleep as
well as he used to, he didn't like to stay out too long at
night. What neighborhood did I live in? Down in the
West Village? That was a wonderful part of town—he
had lived there himself, before he was married, there
were bits of it that had changed so little over the years. I
grew geraniums on my windowsill? And I had a dog—a
pug? How did he enjoy living in the city? Didn't he miss
the countryside?

How comforting it was, to be drawn close by him, to
warm my hands by him at that glittering and chilly party!
We talked about our childhoods at length. He had lost
his mother when he was ten; when I was nine, I had lost
my great-grandmother, to whom I was uncommonly
close, who had only to leave the room for my world to
go black. She—born in 1890—was more mother than
grandmother to me, but what was more, she was of the
same age and generation and general disposition as Mr.
Maxwell's own lost mother. (Later, when I read *They*

Came Like Swallows, I would recognize a painfully exact echo of my own love and grief in Bunny's loss.) So— though Mr. Maxwell and I were over half a century apart—we had not only been shaped by a similar hand, but the same tragedy had befallen us both like the blow of an axe, at strangely the same time, dividing our child-hoods violently into Before and After. I had never really gotten over it, nor had he.

"One carries the mark all one's life. I suppose it's what makes people writers," he said. "Look at Virginia Woolf. In an artist's childhood, there's almost always something missing, isn't there?"

Despite the considerable difference in our ages, my own small-town childhood in Mississippi had been in many respects not very different at all from his, in cen-tral Illinois. We were both shy, non-athletic children, a little too sensitive sometimes and quick to tears; we had grown up in similar houses (high ceilings, ornate Victorian furniture, creaky noises late at night) in simi-lar towns (tree-shaded streets, courthouse square, visits to the cemetery on Sunday afternoons after church). The Illinois Central Railroad had run through my town, too, and was as much a part of my childhood as his. We both had traveling salesmen in the family (his father; my grandfather). We'd grown up with extended family close by, in and out of the houses of uncles and aunts (and neighbors, unrelated by blood, whom one called Uncle and Aunt). I told him I'd kept notebooks when I was a little girl (look of surprise and delight crossing his face) but that all I'd been interested in writing down, as a ten year old, was who I played with at recess and what I ate for dinner.

"But how marvelous to know that now!" he said. "What you ate for dinner when you were ten years old!"

I must have seemed like a baby to him; when he spoke to me, his manner was that of a kind and careful adult to an intelligent child, and yet, in some ways, it was also the candor of a child talking to another child on the playground for the first time. Do you like this? Do you like that? Me, too! Me, too! We found that we both liked to write before breakfast, and that we both liked to stay in our bathrobes and pyjamas until noon. We had both read the writer Lafcadio Hearn when we were growing up. Who reads Lafcadio Hearn now? Yet we had both loved him ("he had a glass eye," said Mr. Maxwell, "did you know that?") and we also shared a love for *Treasure Island,* which we had both read doggedly over and over. There were bits of *Treasure Island* we loved so much that we knew them by heart, not exactly the same bits, but almost exactly, and—as if we were comparing marbles in the schoolyard—we each pulled out our own favorites, the ones we particularly loved, and showed them to each other: old blind Pew staggering enraged and grappling out on the road; violent Billy Bones, drunk at the Admiral Benbow, "singing his ugly old sea-song," and the curious West Indian shells which Jim and his mother find—among other things—in Billy Bones' sea-chest after his murder. "It has often set me thinking since that he should have carried about these shells with him in his wandering, guilty, and hunted life." And then, of course, there was old Ben Gunn. "Many's the long night I've dreamed of cheese—"

"Toasted, mostly!" said Mr. Maxwell, finishing the line for me.

As it happened, I was going to France in a few weeks, so we talked about France, too, and how much we loved it. The first time he'd seen France, he told me, he was forty years old, and he had loved every single moment of every day. He was interested to learn that my dog was coming to France with me—indeed, had accompanied me to France twice before—and laughed when I told him how, when I brought the dog along with me to a restaurant, waiters would escort the pair of us tenderly to a romantic table for two. And he told me how—all over France—he and Emily were always looking everywhere for a château she remembered as a child, and could never find again. He described the château to me in great detail, the same château that's described in the novel of the same name, actually (Emily at this point turning to us, joining in now, all smiles) and I told them I would look for it when I was there. (And I did, too. But I didn't find it. I still wonder if I'll run across it someday.)

And then Emily stood up, and then it was time for them to go—the first guests to leave the party. "Emily," I said, standing myself, "Mr. Maxwell—"

"Oh, don't call me Mr. Maxwell—please call me Bill." He took my hand. "Mr. Maxwell makes me feel so old."

• • •

THE LAST TIME I saw him, it was a cold, miserable day in January and he was crossing York Avenue toward his apartment on Eighty-sixth Street. I was crossing York Avenue the other way, heading west. We passed each other (he was preoccupied, leaning into the wind, holding a paper bag from the corner drugstore with one hand and, with the other, holding his hat onto his head); he didn't see me. If the weather hadn't been so awful, I would have stopped to say hello. We'd corresponded (I have the extraordinarily kind letter he wrote me about my first novel framed and hanging on the wall of my office, to cheer me up on what he himself described to me as "days of lowered consequence") and he and Emily had also been kind enough to show up at a reading I did, at Books and Company on Madison Avenue, not too long before the store closed. But what had made me feel far closer to him than any of this: my love for his work had deepened over the years, to the point where it was almost impossible for me to believe we had ever been in the same room together. For his books exude a quiet calm and charm which is peculiarly their own; almost no other author of the twentieth century presents such passionate emotional depth married to such sublety and artfulness of expression, such exquisite renderings of the texture of life. I think that it was partly this very love for his work that made me suspicious of my motives for wanting to stop him on the street. I didn't want to bother him: an old man in his nineties, struggling across the street with a worried look on his face. (Emily must have been sick then from the cancer which would kill her, though I didn't know it.) I knew he would stop to talk, happily, yet I didn't want to presume on his natural kindness by making him stand around in the cold any longer than he absolutely had to. So I walked by without saying anything. I was sorry the moment I did it—in fact, I felt like running back to catch him, but of course I didn't—and now I'm even sorrier, because I never saw him again.

The irony, of course, is that Mr. Maxwell (I could never bring myself to call him Bill) wrote so profoundly about such moments: the mis-steps that we see only too clearly in hindsight, the accidents and thoughtless failures that crystallize into fate. Even *The Château,* Maxwell's most light-hearted novel, is full of these little accidents, these missed connections and misunderstandings which elsewhere in his work are explored in all their moral complexity. For all Austin's good intentions in *Time Will Darken It,* his efforts to be kind to his young cousin backfire horribly. After Elizabeth Morison's death, of influenza, in *They Came Like Swallows,* Elizabeth's husband and sons are haunted by guilt; each believes himself to have been the unwitting agent of her exposure to the flu. The narrator of "Over By the River" is distressed by the fact that he never once spoke to a neighborhood woman who committed suicide, even though he saw her every day. ("He could have stopped just once, but he hadn't. When the window was open he could have called out to her, even if it was only 'Good morning,' or 'Isn't it a beautiful day?'") And then, of course, there's *So Long, See You Tomorrow*—

which, at its heart, arises from an incident which with many people would be easily forgotten: a friend who passes by another friend, without speaking. The memory, years later, was enough to make Mr. Maxwell wince; but it was a stitch in his psyche which—silently, in darkness, over a long stretch of time—somehow gathered the light to itself and changed into a pure pearl.

And in the end, this may be the quality which I admire about him most as a writer: not his psychological sensitivity, not his beautifully observed detail, not even his sure hand at crafting a sentence (there aren't many American writers of the twentieth century who can turn a sentence as elegantly as he can), but his emotional fearlessness. Though he is the gentlest of novelists, he never averts his gaze from suffering, and his refusal to be consoled by conventional religious hope is as implacable as the fiercest existentialist's. "I grieve," he said in one of his letters, "for everybody who was ever born." Yet his fiction conveys above all the conviction that the world—despite mutability, cruelty, loss, and death—is somehow still a good place. One imagines him stepping out into the dark after Emily, his hand to his heart, unafraid.

Oh, Mr. Maxwell! If I saw you on the street today, I'd stop and tell you all sorts of things! I'd tell you that the little allée of fruit trees in the park near your apartment is in bloom now. That your friend Sylvia the pharmacist and I had a lovely conversation about you in the drugstore the other day. And that I ate a chocolate ice-cream cone at your memorial service—which was certainly the most cheerful memorial service I've ever attended, with the pony, and the balloons, and the music, and the ice-cream cart, and Emily's drawings displayed in the church, and a peacock belonging to St. John the Divine strutting about aggressively at the feet of the funeral guests after the service was over.

I'd tell you, too, that well after you'd died—when I was editing my second novel—I wanted desperately to talk to you, and lay awake in the dark wondering: *What would Mr. Maxwell say? What would he tell me to do?* It seemed to me that you were the only person in the world—living or dead—who could tell me what I needed to know, and I would have dragged out the Ouija board or even resorted to the dark arts if I'd thought it would put me in touch with you for a few minutes. Then one night I awoke from a sound sleep and rose from bed like a sleepwalker and pulled one of your books off the shelf and opened it at random, and your plain sensible answer to my question leapt right out at me: clear, succinct, as pointed and pertinent to my situation as if you'd spoken it directly in my ear. Alec Wilkinson, who has written beautifully about your final days, says that you told him when you were gone, you intended to stay gone—but if I could tell you anything, I'd love most of all to tell you this: that I can hear you talking even now, in your wise, kind voice, though you've been away from the apartment on Eighty-sixth Street for a good while now.

Alice Munro

Maxwell

I FIRST READ William Maxwell sometime in the early sixties. *They Came Like Swallows* was the first novel of his I read, and not long after that, *The Folded Leaf.* I knew right away that this was a good writer, but I don't think I knew how good. I was reading a lot of Big Books then, and I probably didn't have the sense to appreciate someone whose material seemed so familiar—it's not far from Illinois to Ontario, after all, and the people who live there aren't much different, and families are families (or so I thought, not realizing that this has remained a most durably fascinating subject since Cain and Abel), and the desperation of a shy adolescent was nothing new to me.

Years later I read *So Long, See You Tomorrow* (published in 1980), and by that time I knew what I was reading. I went back and reread the novels I had read before, together with *Time Will Darken It* and all the short stories I could find. And I thought: So this is how it should be done. I thought: If only I could go back and write again every single thing that I have written. Not that my writing would, or should, imitate his, but that it might be informed with his spirit.

The foreword to the novel *Time Will Darken It* is a long quotation from a sixteenth-century painter, Francisco Pacheco:

> The order observed in painting a landscape . . . is as follows: First, one draws it, dividing it into three or four distances or planes. In the foremost, where one places the figure or saint, one draws the largest trees or rocks. . . . In the second, smaller trees and houses are drawn; in the third yet smaller, and in the fourth, where the mountain ridges meet the sky, one ends with the greatest diminution of all.
>
> The drawing is followed by the blocking out or laying in of colours, which some painters are in the habit of doing in black and white, although I deem it better to execute it directly in colour. . . . If you temper the necessary quantity of pigment . . . with linseed or walnut oil and add enough white, you shall produce a bright tint. It must not be dark; on the contrary, it must be rather on the light side because time will darken it. . . .

There are two more paragraphs of straightforward, practical instruction, but this is enough to show you what you may take to be Maxwell's intention. Is he not letting you know, here, how he will write his novel? His method will be orderly and deliberate, painstaking and traditional. To a degree, unsurprising. Or so you think, as you proceed to read. You know where you are with this writer; here is the solid background, the well-developed major and minor characters, some nicely managed shifts in point of view.

And then—how this happens is wonderful—something new is happening. The shift is going rather further than you expect and the structure is open and altered. There's a new exhilaration, as if you're walking on air. And with that change in the way the novel is made, there has come a change in what it is about.

It has started off as the story of a youngish, fairly happy Midwestern couple, who are being visited by some relatives from Mississippi. Almost a delicate, but quite realistic, domestic comedy; an evening party, a little rift in the marriage, a too intense young woman, old maids and their mother. But by the end of the book, what has happened? The honourable, only slightly obtuse husband has had to recognize that his notions of how to manage his life are hardly any good at all. The young woman has fallen in love with him and in her desperate state of mind has had a horrible accident. For her scarred face and for her love, there will not be sufficient cure. His wife, going into a dangerous childbirth, is not comforted by his love and perhaps she never will be. He feels cut off from his life. He walks through the town in the dark, to the railway station. And something happens there that no one else will ever know about and that he himself may not be sure about (or perhaps he will be quite sure but will think it just as well to tell himself he isn't). All that is involved, physically, is (probably) that he waited a little too long a little too close to the track, and jumped out of harm's way when the stationmaster called out to warn him. But in his own mind or somehow by his own wish he has fallen, he has been swimming as if underwater straight toward the train's light and then the train is above him and he is being rolled over and over on the gravel. He feels foolish— after all he was not ready to die. But nothing can be done now, it's all over, he believes that he is in a death trap he cannot escape.

But he is still there, still alive, watching the lights on the last car of the train receding from him, getting smaller and smaller.

This passage is done with great care and intensity, so that we feel the intensity but not the care. It is seamless, perfect. A man tries or doesn't quite try to kill himself. This happens or that happens, but in the end here is what really happens:

> *I should have waited for another train, maybe, but I didn't. I was very tired. I don't ever remember being as tired as I was that night. I'd been letting myself down. A little bit at a time, over a period of several hours I guess, I'd been letting myself down. I'd been watching what other people do,*

so I could learn to be more like them, and somehow—maybe because I didn't understand what I saw or it could have been that I was just too tired—it didn't seem worth the bother. I don't know how I got home. I just found myself there, looking through the dining-room window at the thermometer to see how cold it was, turning off the lights, going up the stairs to bed.

A couple of weeks later his wife, Martha, comes home from the hospital with their new son. The girl has gone away, wrecked and defeated. The marriage is safe. Lying in bed beside her husband, the wife begins to tell him about a feeling of change she has, in fact a loss of faith in their life together. In the midst of this he goes to sleep.

She gets up then, feeling anger, and then hopelessness. She sits by the window holding her baby, thinking how she will leave him, taking her children with her, how she longs to begin a life that is poor and decent and brave. Looking down at her son she thinks how she will bring him up to be unlike his father; not to be nice, not to be polite, not to compromise and make the best of things, she will bring him up in full knowledge of what life is. Finally, cold, but still wakeful and angry, she gets back into bed.

Austin stirred, and put his arm across her, and she took hold of it, by the wrist, and removed it, but when she moved away from him, towards the outer edge of the bed, he followed again in his sleep, and curled around her in a way that made her want to shout at him, and beat his face with her fists. She pushed the arm away, roughly this time, but he still did not waken. The arm had a life of its own. All the rest of him, his body and his soul, were asleep. But 'the arm was awake, and came across her, and the hand settled on her heart, and she let it stay there for a moment, thinking how hard and heavy it was compared to the child she had been holding, how importunate, how demanding; how it was no part of her and never would be, insisting on a satisfaction, even in sleep, that she could not give. She started to push it away once more but her own arms were bound to the bed. Only her mind was awake, able to act, to hate. And then suddenly the delicate gold chain of awareness, no stronger than its weakest link, gave way. Circled by the body next to her, enclosed in warmth, held by the arm that knew (even though the man it belonged to did not), Martha King was asleep.

Here again the most ruthless revelation, made with such quiet confidence and lack of fuss, the opposites of married life—of life—laid side by side like Austin and Martha. This is true; that is true.

A little while before this, when Martha entered the hospital, the nurse took her to a room at a distance from other patients, saying it would make for less disturbance. Still ignorant of what was to come, Martha said that their noise would not have bothered her. And the nurse said that was not what she had been thinking about. She had been thinking about how the noise that Martha will have to make will affect them.

This shocking, even brutal surprise is delivered so matter-of-factly and naturally that Martha might almost miss it, though she doesn't. The surprise of the story is delivered in somewhat the same way. The shock, the dramatic and tragic point, might seem to be the girl's accident. If you were trying to tell people what happens in the book, that is what you might tell them about. But the deeper and when you look back on it the more disturbing surprise is what is revealed about these two unexceptional people, Austin and Martha, about their separateness and their bond and the marriage that will certainly continue and may in the end be judged happier than most.

In the novels *They Came Like Swallows* and *The Folded Leaf,* the material close to the writer's heart makes its naked appearance, and henceforth he is not going to bother much with anything else.

They Came Like Swallows is about the life of a young family and the way in which that life is shattered by the death of the mother. This story is told again and again in Maxwell's fiction, in stories that seem autobiographical but may not be as autobiographical as they seem—and there is something new with each telling, some new action at the periphery or revelation near the centre, a different light or shading, a discovery, as there must be in the stories at the heart of our lives, stories that grow and change as we do and never go away.

In *The Folded Leaf* two adolescent boys are turning into men, and the friendship between them is turning into something they cannot bear. It is done with great care and quietness and a peculiar sense of honour. By that I suppose I mean that tragedy or—as it turns out, near tragedy—seems to take shape so naturally and inevitably, and though the shadow is lifted, the threat is gone for the present, there is the sense that in this boy's life, it can never be gone for good.

So Long, See You Tomorrow was written many years later than these two novels. But there again is the friendship of two boys—much younger boys this time—and the friendship's betrayal. There is also the breaking of the family upon the death of the mother, the wounds inflicted in an almost random way among the survivors of her death, and the separate efforts of those survivors to go on living.

This material Maxwell has treated well before, but never so well as here, never with so wide a vision. For this story does not stand on its own, it is fitted together with another story, a classic story of adultery, of inappropriate, helpless, destructive sexual passion. And the outcome here is darker than in the earlier novels, with their escapes from suicide and their humbled reconciliations. Here there is a murder, and then a suicide—and not a hope, things having gone so far, that this suicide should fail. The drama is familiar and the tragedy predictable, as much so to the readers of daily newspapers as to the readers of great novels, but there are unexpected pauses and asides. The central actors in the drama seem at times to be stalling, to be looking for a way out, trying to escape playing their roles all the way through. It's as if they can't quite believe what is happening.

And while the tragedy is stalled at the centre, its ripples widen out. We enter the life of the housekeeper hired by the man who is waiting—without understanding that he is waiting—to be murdered. She would like a little conversation. We meet the owner of the farm—this is a countryside of tenant farmers—a hard-bitten no-nonsense woman who happens to be a bit sweet on this particular manly tenant. And we get to know the old woman who has given shelter to the wife and children of the man who will commit the murder. We discover what it's like inside the narrow plain little house that is her pride and solace, and which is now filled with the circling complaints and fears of that man's wife and the silent misery of his son.

We also enter the life of a dog—the dog who has been left behind on the farm when this family broke apart. She is supposed to become the property of the new tenant, but she happens to possess the sort of affections that cannot be transferred:

> The borrowed Model T drive off down the lane . . . with night coming on, and no lights in the house, and no smoke going up the chimney.
> She waited a long long time, trying not to worry. Trying to be good—trying to be especially good. And telling herself that they had only gone in to town and

were coming right back, even though it was perfectly obvious that this wasn't true. Not the way they acted. Eventually, in spite of her, the howls broke out. Sitting on her haunches, with her muzzle raised to the night sky, she howled and howled. And it wasn't just the dog howling, it was all the dogs she was descended from, clear back to some wolf or other.

She heard footsteps and was sure it was the boy: *He had heard her howling and come from wherever it was he had been all this time and was going to rescue her. . . .*

It turned out to be the man's friend from over the way. He put his lantern on the ground and untied her and talked to her and stroked her ears, and for a minute or two everything was all right. But then she remembered how they didn't tell her to get in the car with them but drove off without even a backward look, and she let out another despairing howl.

The man who is going to be murdered gets her some scraps to eat and some water, and finally takes her home with him, and she waits there until the new tenant—the young man who is taking over the farm of the man who will be a murderer—arrives and claims her:

Seeing the rope dangling from the tree, James Walker kept the dog tied up for the next two days. . . . But he also fed her and saw that her pan had water in it and talked to her sometimes. And when night came there was a light in the kitchen window, and the dog smelled wood smoke. Things could have been worse. From time to time she wanted to howl, and managed not to. The day after that, trucks came, bringing cattle and hogs and farm machinery and furniture. And that evening the young man untied the rope and said, "Come on, old girl, I need you to help me round up the cows." She understood what he said all right, but she wasn't his old girl, and she lit off down the road as fast as lightning.

It's no use, she won't learn and she won't change, and her true owner, the man she loved, has her put down. His first murder.

This passage is one of the riskiest I can think of, and it is managed without the slightest difficulty. The writer dares to call up again the familiar sentiment of all those faithful-dog stories from books or movies, to write about it at length and with absolute respect. The dog's pain is harsh and real and has its place in the story, just like anybody else's pain.

There is a narrator of this story. He vanishes for long periods of time but he never lets go. He is the temporary friend of the boy that dog was waiting for—the son of the suicide, the murderer. During that period of waiting, before the murder or the suicide happen, the two boys get into the habit of meeting after school and climbing up into the skeleton of the new house that the narrator's father and stepmother are building. They walk about on the rafters, hardly speaking, perhaps hardly aware of the sense of displacement that brings them together. Each of these boys has behind him a radically altered—and, in a sense, lost—family. In one case the change has been brought about by a death, the death of the mother, and in the other by the love of two people who are married to other people, a love now practically swallowed up in the desperation it has brought to everybody involved, and their growing sense of the threat of cataclysm to follow. Naturally this is nothing they can mention.

Quite early in the book the narrator, grown old, has been looking at a sculpture in the Museum of Modern Art. It is *The Palace at 4 A.M.* by Giacometti. A spare, strange structure of thin uprights and horizontal beams, in which there is something like a flying bird, the backbone of an animal, a female figure, and a hollowed-out spatulate shape with a ball in front of it. He is reminded of that house that his father was building for himself and the woman who has replaced the boy's mother. He quotes from the artist's own words on his work:

"This object took shape little by little in the late summer of 1932; it revealed itself to me slowly, the various parts taking their exact form and their precise place within the whole. By autumn it had attained such reality that its actual execution in space took no more than one day. It is related without any doubt to a period in my life that had come to an end a year before, when for six whole months hour after hour was passed in the company of a woman who, concentrating all life in herself, magically transformed my every moment. We used to construct a fantastic palace at night . . . a very fragile palace of matchsticks. At the slightest false move a whole section of this tiny construction would collapse. We would always begin it over again. I don't know why it came to be inhabited by a spinal column in a cage—the spinal column this woman sold me one of the very first nights I met her on the street—and by one of the skeleton birds that she saw the very night before the morning in which our life together collapsed—the skeleton birds that flutter with cries of joy at four o'clock in the morning very high above the pool of clear, green water where the extremely fine, white skeletons of fish float in the great unroofed hall. . . . On the other side there appeared the statue of a woman, in which I recognize my mother, just as she appears in my earliest memories. . . ."

Giacometti. The relationships of a middle-class family in town and of two tenant-farmer families out in the country, on adjoining farms. A perfect friendship turned into enmity by an overpowering love. The mostly inarticulate life of boys. The unhelpful workings of the legal system and the eddies of news and gossip in a small town. The secret feelings of several people who are not perhaps essential to the story but are of interest to the reader. The struggle of a man long grown to accept the blow dealt to him when he was a child. The not-so-secret—and fatal—emotional attachments of a dog. All this in a book 135 pages long, with no crowding. Everything given its due. Everything arranged with such skill that there doesn't seem to be any skill to it at all. Nothing but easy, natural storytelling. Something to say about this matter of story-telling, as well:

> I seem to remember that I went to the new house one winter day and saw snow descending through the attic to the upstairs bedrooms. It could also be that I never did any such thing, for I am fairly certain that in a snapshot album I have lost track of there was a picture of the house taken in the circumstances I have just described, and it is possible that I am remembering that rather than an actual experience. What we, or at any rate what I, refer to confidently as memory—meaning a moment, a scene, a fact that has been subjected to a fixative and thereby rescued from oblivion—is really a form of storytelling that goes on continually in the mind and often changes with the telling. Too many conflicting emotional interests are involved for life ever to be wholly acceptable, and possibly it is the work of the story-teller to rearrange things so that they conform to this end. In any case, in talking about the past we lie with every breath we draw.

I have been quoting at considerable length, I know it. My only excuse is that it has been such a joy, and some-thing like a renewal of hope, to let the words and sen-tences of this writer flow through my mind and my fingertips.

Paula Fox

A Story in the Dark

I READ WILLIAM MAXWELL'S early novel, *The Folded Leaf,* in 1951 in Wellfleet, Massachusetts, where I was living then. Its range of feeling, its bittersweet evocation of youth, the way the language didn't preen, even subtly, which would have sabotaged its own meaning, but rather by its simplicity deepened the meaning, stirred me. I thought of Chekhov. I recall little else I read that year.

Thirty-three years later, I met William Maxwell. We had both arrived early in the evening for an arts award ceremony, sponsored by Brandeis University, that was being held in the auditorium of the Guggenheim Museum.

For fifteen minutes or so, we were the only people there, in a glass projection booth above the auditorium's rows of seats. As I walked in, he came forward and introduced himself and shook my hand. When I spoke my name, his expression conveyed that he knew about me, and what he knew was all to the good.

We were both to receive fiction awards, he the Brandeis Medal and I, a citation. Between 1951 and 1984, I had read many of his books, and his stories in *The New Yorker,* where he was an editor.

I now know he had a genius for intimacy, a genius for making one feel singular and worthy and interesting, even, as I was to learn in the years that followed, in rooms full of other people.

We began to talk. He had been cleaning out the attic of his house in the country that afternoon, and he went into rueful, comic detail. I told him about a letter I had received that morning from a fifteen-year-old high school student who attended classes on Long Island.

She had read a book of mine, *The Slave Dancer.* Her teacher had given her the assignment of writing to me about the story. In her letter she noted that her only reason for writing me was the teacher's order. She had two questions: Why had I written the book? Did I have a slave?

I recalled that I had replied to the student with uncommon irony. Perhaps, I had suggested in the letter, she would come across the Emancipation Proclamation of January 1, 1863, in her history studies.

Bill threw back his narrow beautiful head and laughed. Encouraged, I went on to tell him how that same day my husband, Martin Greenberg, who taught literature to college students, had come home with yet another tale. In his afternoon class that same day, he had been seized by an irresistible impulse. When was Jesus born? he asked his students. There were a few giggles, and one young man raised his hand. "The seventeenth century?" he asked hopefully.

During the ceremony all those who were to receive awards sat in camp chairs on a raised platform to the audience's right, like actors who had answered a casting call. Just before the playwright Edward Albee called my name, a minute's dramatization of one of my novels flashed upon a screen.

Although Bill, sitting beside me, touched my hand and whispered, "Don't look!" I had already stolen a glance. A woman was shown standing by a window, weeping, while outside the rain poured down. Bill had been right. It meant nothing at all.

After the ceremony, after drinks in the museum, Bill and his wife, Emmy, Martin and I, among others, trooped along Fifth Avenue to a dinner party at someone's apartment. Bill was merry and expansive but without a touch of triumph. Never that. He carried his fame lightly.

Martin and I spent other evenings at other dinner parties with the Maxwells. Two of them stay with me. One was at the New York City apartment of Francis Steegmuller and his wife, Shirley Hazzard. It was an intense, concentrated, and effortless gathering. When we all stood at the door to say good night, it seemed as if no time had passed since our arrival. The second was a party which still whirls around me. Out of its spinning center, Bill suddenly appeared and sat down on the sofa beside me.

"Why don't we write to one another?" he asked.

To my unending regret, I didn't follow up on his suggestion. Perhaps it was because I felt too abashed that I didn't write to him. What a loss!

In the spring of 1996 I flew with my husband to Israel. On the late evening of our first day there, while walking toward the Mishkenot Sha'ananim, the place where we were staying in Jerusalem, I was assaulted by a figure in the dark who fled with my pocketbook and all it contained. He knocked me to the stony ground.

An Israeli friend who was with us found a strolling couple on the street who had a cell phone, and the police and an ambulance were called.

I spent a month in the hospital, three weeks in Jerusalem, one week in Columbia-Presbyterian in New York City. The hospital stay was followed by nearly a year of convalescence. Seven years later, I still experience short periods when I have difficulty speaking.

During the spring or fall of the following year, I can't recall which, Martin and I went to the Brooklyn Academy of Music where, in one of its theaters, we saw a production of *The Steward of Christendom*.

During the matinee intermission, we were standing in an aisle in the loge. I looked around and saw in a distant aisle below Bill Maxwell speaking animatedly with a young couple.

In the shadowed dark, his white hair gleamed like a

beacon. I said his name. Bill. It was nearly all I could say at the time. Seeing him suddenly like that made me speechless. I said his name more loudly as I began to walk down to him. He turned, smiling. As I came nearer, he held out his hands to me. I went down a few more steps. Bill, I repeated and repeated. He had either heard from Shirley Hazzard about my Israel misadventure or he saw and sensed my agitation. Whatever he knew, he introduced me to the young couple, holding my hand all the while. And I was able to smile at him, although I still couldn't speak. The lights went on signaling the intermission was over, and I returned to my husband.

It was the last time I saw Bill.

"When we were first married," he writes in the preface to *All the Days and Nights,* a collection of his short stories, "after we had gone to bed I would tell her a story in the dark."

That is where most of us tell our stories.

Michael Collier

The Dog Gets to Dover: William Maxwell as a Correspondent

ONE OF THE LAST things that William Maxwell wrote and published was a short essay for a Festschrift celebrating Eudora Welty's ninetieth birthday. The essay took the form of a letter. "Eudora dear," it begins, "I have been thinking how fortunate we were to have been born toward the end of the first decade of this century." What follows is a lyrical though factual list of what the America of that decade was like: "To begin with, the quiet, except on the Fourth of July. No heavy trucks, no bulldozers, no power lawnmowers. . . . The grass was full of wonderful things—spring beauties, dandelions, the one-winged seeds of the maple trees . . . sometimes a piece of tinfoil or a penny." "If there was a red light in the sky," Maxwell reminds Welty, "you picked up the telephone receiver and asked Central where the fire was and she knew."

It is fitting that one of the last pieces William Maxwell published not only recalled the period of the century in which most of his own fiction was grounded but was a "letter" to a writer he befriended through his work as a fiction editor of *The New Yorker*. During his life not only did literary correspondences give him great pleasure to read but he himself was a prodigious correspondent, whether it be with family and friends or with the writers he worked with at *The New Yorker*. In the special collections of the University of Illinois-Urbana Library, Maxwell's archive of correspondence is massive and includes John Updike, Louise Bogan, John Cheever, Peter Taylor, Harold Brodkey, Kay Boyle, John O'Hara, Irwin Shaw, Mary McCarthy, Tennessee Williams, and James Thurber, to name a few. Large portions of his letters, such as the correspondence with Robert Fitzgerald and J. D. Salinger (the latter to be kept private, as both writers wished), will eventually form part of the Urbana archive. Once all of his letters reside in the Urbana archive, it will comprise one of the most significant collections of American literary correspondence of the twentieth century and is likely to demonstrate that Maxwell was one of this century's great letter writers.

Already, two collections of his correspondence have been published: *The Happiness of Getting It Down Right: Letters of Frank O'Connor and William Maxwell* (1996) and *The Element of Lavishness: Letters of Sylvia Townsend Warner and William Maxwell,* 1938–1978 (published in 2001, shortly after his death). Maxwell's job at *The New Yorker* put him in a particularly unique position to foster such a wide-ranging correspondence, but this alone does not make his letters unique. What is of paramount importance in defining Maxwell's correspondence is the character of the man who wrote them and his ability to befriend and love people.

In the introduction to his collection of essays and reviews, *The Outermost Dream,* Maxwell wrote, "diaries, memoirs, published correspondence, biography and autobiography—which are what I was asked to consider—do not spring from prestidigitation or require a long apprenticeship. They tell what happened—what people said and did and wore and ate and hoped for and were afraid of, and in detail after often unimaginable detail they refresh our idea of existence and hold oblivion at arms length." That Maxwell was attracted to the letters of literary figures, as well as their biographies, memoirs, and journals, is made clear by the fact that he agreed only to review examples of these for *The New Yorker.* The last review essay Maxwell published with the magazine, in 1994, covered the first two volumes of *The Letters of Robert Louis Stevenson.*

. . .

ROLAND BARTHES, in his essay "Deliberation," cites four types of motives for the keeping of a journal: poetic, historical, utopian, and amorous. The "amorous" motive constitutes the "journal as a workshop of sentences: not of 'fine phrases' but of correct ones," in which language refines the "exactitude of the speech according to an enthusiasm . . . a fidelity of intention which greatly resembles passion." Letter writing, too, can take the form of a journal. Maxwell once said of his correspondence with O'Connor, "letter writing for me was a little like keeping a journal." The "amorous," especially in its exactitude, enthusiasm, and passion, is everywhere present in the letters of William Maxwell. Writing to Sylvia Townsend Warner in April 1958, he declared, "I have often thought that we were meant for each other—you to write to me and I to read you. . . . every sentence I have ever read of yours gave me immediate intense pleasure—at the world as you saw it, and at how you said what you were saying—the intense pleasure of appreciating a personal style." Although Maxwell and Warner met only twice during their lives, they were in such constant contact through letters that Maxwell once told her, "The only person I really see a great deal of, among all my friends, is Sylvia" (April 1961).

Similar to his relationship with Sylvia Townsend Warner, Maxwell's relationship with Frank O'Connor started when he began editing the writer's stories for *The New Yorker.* In *The Happiness of Getting It Down Right,* it is easy to follow the progress of an editor working with his writer to the formation of an unshakable friendship. When Maxwell queries Frank O'Connor in 1947 about a story of his the magazine was going to publish, he addresses him as Mr. O'Connor, a formality that continues until 1954, when he begins to address him as

O'Connor. This creeping intimacy affords him the opportunity to report in the same letter, "Last week end we went out to our house in the country, to see a man about digging a deeper well, and the first daffodil points were foolishly above the ground. In town it is very springlike, and deceptive. The kind of weather that leads young men (or did me) to fall in love with girls they don't marry." By 1955, they greet each other as Frank and Bill. In 1957, O'Connor, giving up his pseudonym—his real name was Michael John O'Donovan—refers to himself as Michael, and by the next year they each begin to sign off their letters with "love."

Once Maxwell had established a friendly intimacy with Warner and O'Connor, he extended and deepened the intimacy by writing to other members of their households. Eventually, he writes to Warner's lover Valentine, to Harriet (O'Connor's wife), and to O'Connor's daughter, Hallie-Og. And Emmy, Maxwell's wife, writes to them as well. The tone of the letters becomes familial, and the friendships collaborative and collective. Successes and failures, deaths and illnesses, holidays and inconsequential days, insights and perplexities are all shared as easily as breath. What's most striking is how unguarded and fresh the exchanges seem. Even so, one doesn't feel as if everything going on in their lives is discussed, but that a general stoicism, typical of Maxwell's generation, is in operation, filtering out what would be considered private and proprietary. Nevertheless, the emotion the letters convey is authentic and deep.

While the "amorous" nature of Maxwell's relationships with Warner and O'Connor is similar, the tone of the letters is markedly different. When writing Warner, Maxwell speaks from that part of himself, he once confessed to her, that as a little boy preferred the company of women. With O'Connor, he is more direct, chummy, and playfully competitive. "An egotist I certainly am," he writes to O'Connor in 1961, who was recovering from surgery on his hand. "Didn't I rush off, two days after I got your letter, and have a lump removed from my shoulder, just so you wouldn't get ahead of me." Partly what we hear is the conversation of two family men, discussing their wives and children, living arrangements, the vexation of not finding time to work, and partly we hear Maxwell playing the role of editor and nudge. "Scold, scold, scold, how boring Protestants are," he tells his friend in 1963, after urging him to sharpen the focus in a piece he is working on. While Maxwell as editor is everywhere evident in his correspondence with O'Connor ("I don't know why I badger you so much," he writes later that year), intimacy and affection break through constantly. "It's strange to think of last Sunday's sleet beating against the windows of your forsaken apartment," he writes when O'Connor is away from New York. "Do you ever think how much the objects miss you? Or how much I do?"

Maxwell was never interested in keeping a journal, though he did attempt one during his apprenticeship years. Harold, one of the protagonists in his novel *The Château,* notices that his wife is keeping a diary of their trip through France and thinks, "She had a façade that she retired behind . . . the image of an unworldly, well-bred, charming-looking, gentle young woman. The image was not even false to her character; it merely left out half of it. . . . It was the façade that was keeping the diary." Thomas Mallon, in *A Book of One's Own: People and Their Diaries,* points out that diaries are the only form of writing to which the verb "keep" is applied: "One doesn't 'keep' a poem or a letter or a novel. . . . But diaries are . . . about the preservation and protection of the self." In conversation, Maxwell once told me that his disinclination for keeping a diary came from the dual tedium produced by writing to one's self and for a future, unknown reader. The necessity of having someone to whom his writing was addressed was as true for Maxwell as it was for Sylvia Townsend Warner, whom he described as needing "to write for an audience, a specific person, in order to bring out her pleasure in enchanting."

• • •

MY OWN CORRESPONDENCE with William Maxwell began in 1981, after I had dinner at his East Eighty-sixth Street apartment as a guest of William Meredith, who had been my teacher in college. Several years earlier, I had been introduced to Maxwell's work when Meredith told me that he had been the ghostwriter of the jacket copy for Meredith's 1975 book of poems *Hazard the Painter.* I was a sophomore in college then, and it was made clear to me that I was meant to keep the bones of this knowledge buried. As an acolyte to this secret, I felt as if I had an intimacy with Maxwell even before I met him.

At dinner I met his wife, Emmy, and Brookie, his daughter, who is close to my age. The evening was courteous, but what I remember most is the sincerity and intimacy the Maxwells produced by the quiet force of their presence. Sitting in their living room, we talked about poetry, mainly, and Bill would occasionally go to the bookshelf and take out Yeats or Hardy or a volume by someone else whose name came up, and we would take turns reading. This went on before and after the meal. It sounds a little like the way hymns are sung at church, but it wasn't like that at all. Reverence was not the overriding mood; it was more like a desire to put what one cares about directly into the ears of those one loves.

A few weeks later, in response to a thank-you note I had sent from California, where I was living, I received a postcard with a single sentence echoing my own pleasure with the evening. It also included their New York and Yorktown Heights telephone numbers and an invitation to call the next time I was in the city. From 1981 to 1987, we exchanged letters occasionally, perhaps four or five times a year, but after April 1987, when Bill and Emmy stayed with my wife and me in Baltimore after a reading Bill had given at the University of Maryland, where I taught, the frequency of our correspondence increased to meet the needs of a friendship that to my own bewilderment (Bill was my senior by almost fifty years) began to deepen.

Among the many remarkable things I learned about letter writing from William Maxwell during my years of corresponding with him, these stand out. No letter should ever go unanswered. Receiving a letter in which illness or personal difficulty are mentioned requires not only a response containing a remedy or solution but a follow-up phone call. Books, writing, reading, and childhood are paramount topics, followed by wives, children, and friends, and then in no particular order cats, dogs, birds, gardens, domestic arrangements, music, museums and their current exhibitions, and in general whatever else might create delight and pleasure in the reader. I was to learn that what one should live for more than anything else are small moments of overwhelming astonishment. "[A]ll pleasure," he wrote to Sylvia Townsend Warner in January 1961, "is got . . . from the rubbing off of somebody else's pleasure in something. From eye to eye and skin to skin. A cousin of love-making."

Maxwell believed that "The personal correspondence of writers feeds off left-over energy." This produces a feeling of "lavishness" because, as he noted, "the chances of any given letter's surviving is fifty-fifty at most." It also produces a feeling "of confidence—of the relaxed backhand stroke that can place the ball anywhere that it pleases the writer to have it go." Typical of the kind of lavishness he could produce is this, in a letter to Warner in September 1966: "If you are lucky, you find yourself in the field where the flower is growing. You don't buy tickets for it. Dear old, old friend, tiredness one gets over, but don't allow permanent melancholy in the house." And a typical moment of confidence, also in a letter to Warner, September 1958: "The peach tree has its first crop, of white peaches that taste like nectarines. The roses are about to bloom once more, and they'd better hurry. The cloud compositions are the best in years. And both children have had their hair cut, which always has the effect of putting them in quotation marks for a few days."

Maxwell wanted characters in fiction to sound like real people, not caricatures. As a result snippets of conversation O'Connor might report, such as the woman in Dublin who says, "Oh, sir, I can't sleep at night with my mind," thrilled him. Maxwell peppered his own letters with the speech and idiom of his native Midwest. To Warner he admits that phrases he heard his Aunt Edith use, such as "crazy as Dick's hatband," astonished him because their "explanation seemed over the hill of Time, beyond recovering." I remember when "crazy as Dick's hatband" showed up puzzlingly in a letter he sent to me, as well as other idioms and figures of speech. Phrases that pop up not only in my letters from Maxwell but in those he sent to Warner and O'Connor as well might include "And I am never one to paint instead of going to my mother's funeral"; "Well, leg over leg and the dog gets to Dover"; "I will keep my eye on the cork and report any bobbing"; or "this will make [him] morbid or I don't know Arkansas." Not only do they carry an idiomatic vividness, but they are indicative of Maxwell's habit of metaphoric thinking, a habit that has its origins in the way people talked and was therefore alive in a way that was practical and useful. Whenever I came across one of these phrases in a letter, it seemed like a found poem.

.   .   .

JUST AS NABOKOV liked to illustrate his lectures, Bill, who had once been an art student, might include a drawing in a letter. He once sketched a walker for Warner when old age and a fall had reduced her to hobbling. He was also an impeccable direction giver. Despite the elaborate directions he once sent me which were meant to lead me from my apartment in New Haven, Connecticut, to their country house in Westchester County, I got supremely turned around and stubbornly lost. When I finally called to get my bearings, there was not only worry in his voice but contrition for having failed me. Another time, when I arrived at their Manhattan apartment after they were in bed, and a key had been left for me with the doorman, I found this typed note on the nightstand in the guestroom: "Michael: I probably don't need to tell you, to set the alarm you turn the knob in the center of the back of the clock and push down on the bar at the back so that it rises above the level where it now is. There's fresh orange juice in the refrigerator. Sleep well."

Directions, drawings, and notes not only were the result of Bill's fastidious courtesy and manners, but revealed a selfless, worrying preoccupation with the other person. Accompanying the drawing of the walker to Warner was this fretting concern: "I am haunted by the thought of you putting out your hand for a steadying piece of furniture that isn't, as it happens, there. Alas I don't think it [a walker] will do anything for the pain in your legs. Wings is [*sic*] what you really need. Why has it taken me so long to think of it?" The health and well-being of his friends were foremost, but all things being equal, he fretted over whether they were writing. In his letters to O'Connor this worry took the form of playful badgering. "The number of things," he laments, "you can think of to do, the number of talents you can come up with, to keep from writing stories, exceeds all comprehension. . . . But where are those stories that always used to come in threes?"

His habits of paying meticulous attention to the tiniest of details—"the knob in the center of the back of the clock"—are also the extension of his writer's passion for accuracy. Nevertheless, he did not pay attention merely in order to get things right for the page. Accuracy deflected complacency. In older age these habits helped to keep him sharp and focused and engaged in life, and although he was no longer making sentences for stories, he was still writing letters to a wide range of friends. Many of them, like myself, were considerably younger, and so for us his letters contained the wisdom of Solomon spoken with the gentleness of Saint Francis. In 1994 he wrote to me, "either you retire from life or you advance to meet it."

For Maxwell, letters were not merely a way of staying in touch with friends but a means to participate intimately in their lives. His sympathetic powers were so strong that for him reading an account of some incident, in books or letters, nearly equaled the experience itself. When the mother of Valentine Auckland, Warner's lover, died, Bill wrote to Warner, "I loved her. That is, I loved reading about her." Throughout his life, he was deeply affected by books. He read the *Goncourt Journals* a page at a time, and when he finished, he declared to Warner, "all I ask of life is the privilege of being able to read." In 1996 when he was re-reading Keats's letters, he had to stop because, as he wrote me, "I was not ready to let Keats die." And in another letter I received from him, he made this rapturous statement about Marianne Moore: "Reading her prose is like looking at the morning star."

· · ·

TOWARD THE END of his life, reading and writing came together in a kind of painful synesthesia. In the spring of 2000, one of his letters admitted, "I can't find anything to read that isn't overstimulating. I am about half way through *War and Peace* and if I read that after dinner I go on living it in my dreams. Awful things that I know are going to happen, scenes I have made up in my sleep and sometimes just writing." In one of the last interviews he gave, Maxwell said the only thing he would regret about no longer being alive was that he would no longer be able to read—no Chekhov, no Turgenev, no Tolstoy, no Keats.

The ability to live fully in a world created of language is one of the qualities that made him such an insightful and empowering editor. He once wrote to Warner: "It is one of the pleasures of my life, that your stories come directly from you to me. So close does it bring us that I feel as if I could reach out and take the pages as you add the last correction, bunch them together, and decide that it is safe to let go of them." In 1965, he wrote to both O'Connor and Warner about an exhibit of manuscripts by Hawthorne, Crane, Conrad, Woolf, and many others, on display at the New York Public Library. From the seeds of Virginia Woolf's sketchy "plan" of *To the Lighthouse,* Maxwell told O'Connor that he heard "the voice of the novelist talking to himself. In the midst of miracles, the future lying all clear around him, modesty struggling with pride, the work all to come, and farther away still the nagging doubts that will slow the whole thing down and spoil his pleasure after the accomplishment is in hand." The miraculous and magical work of writing was something he believed in with a quiet religiosity. He finished his letter to O'Connor this way: ". . . so it [*To the Lighthouse*] was a literary masterpiece. Though I know I shouldn't, I believe in the life everlasting, and the communion of saints, provided the saints are writers."

When writing about William Maxwell it is easy to make him sound saintly, not because he was a saint, but because his nature was so generous and his conversation and concerns were so highly attenuated—ascetic, really—on the life of art and writing, and because in spite of this asceticism, he was also very much grounded in the world of things and the details of domesticity. He was not unaware of the difficulty his preoccupations might make for those close to him and the sacrifices others were forced to make on his behalf, especially Emmy and his daughters. Nevertheless, he was unrepentant when he confronted this aspect of his life. In response to a complaint of mine about the pressures of writing and teaching, and the effect this had on my wife and sons, he wrote, "that it is not easy to be the child of a writer is something that I'm sure has crossed your mind." And then as if seeing back to a similar panorama that once occupied his own life, he continued, "The past cannot be undone, and it doesn't seem to be easy to draw a line between it and the present. If I had it to do all over again I don't suppose I would change anything. The writer in me would say, how dare you?"

The writer in Maxwell represented an unremitting and unblinking force. In his letters to me, he mostly focused on the rapturous aspects of the creative act, the exaltative energy that carried with it an almost moral urgency about art, and the writers who comprised his lineage—his communion of saints. But behind this, I always felt the pressure of that other, darker energy: the energy that could sometimes seduce by idealizing— "there is nothing about Keats you haven't read"—or praise by exaggeration—"The Odysseus poem is a marvel. I clasp it to me like a person. If you had written only that one poem it would get you into the company of true poets." The goal of this exuberance was not only to inspire others to work at their fullest capacity but to control and pacify through love the powerful emotions that swirled inside of him, right up to the time of his death.

Maxwell did not seek perfection in either life or work. Instead what he found to be achievable was a kind of human capaciousness that was more like a state of being. In his review of Stevenson's letters, he quotes what Hugh Walpole said of Frances Sitwell: "There is nothing you could not tell her. . . . She had to the last that certain stamp of great character, an eager acceptance of the whole life." This state of eager acceptance was one he could recognize in others as well. He described Emmy's ninety-two-year-old father to Warner this way: he "has always been a good letter writer, but his letters have recently taken on a kind of radiance, as if he had stopped taking any ordinary part in life, stopped worrying, I mean, about the outcome of things, and simply looked around him with delight at the way everything is." And of a childhood neighbor he encountered on a trip to Lincoln, Illinois, while researching his memoir, *Ancestors,* he concluded that "in the razor's edge between living and dying herself, she has come to regard everything and everybody as beautiful and miraculous. As indeed they are." Most of my own friendship with Maxwell took place during his ninth and tenth decades, and as a result I can attest to the fact that he had reached a state of marvelous regard for the world. In one of the last letters I received from him, he came to this realization while watching his grandson, Ellis, play in the park: "I was struck by the fact that he didn't express his happiness merely by the look on his face but with his whole body—legs, everything."

Maxwell has been criticized at times for the overly fastidiousness of his life and art. The source of this criticism promotes a fallacy about art, especially twentieth-century art. In part this fallacy says that inner turmoil needs to express itself in external turmoil: manic art equals manic life or vice versa. Or that controlled and orderly surfaces are repressive and untruthful. Maxwell's approach, one consistent with his temperament, was different. He developed a manner of working that allowed him to lock onto a particular frequency of experience and to sharpen the tuning as finely as possible. The result was clarity and definition. Background noise and static were filtered out by his sensibility, which was as acute as Flaubert's and as economical as Chekhov's. The clarity could be as explicit as his memory of the decade he and Eudora Welty were born into, or it could be excruciating. The last time I spoke with Bill was the morning after Emmy died. "There's been a failure in the arrangements," he said. "Harriet is coming this morning to take Emmy to the incinerator, and instead of bringing one body, she should be bringing two." He also told me that while sitting with Emmy, after she had died, he remembered that shortly after his mother's death, more than eighty years before, a man his father did not like for some reason had come to pay his respects at their house. When his father saw who it was, he slammed the door in the man's face. Bill was standing near his father at the time. He told me that he didn't realize anyone, let alone his father, could treat others that way. But what was most vivid about the incident, and what he saw there in the darkness as he sat with Emmy, was snow falling on the man his father had turned away. Later I thought of something he had written to me a few months earlier, in what turned out to be the last letter I received from him: "God knows there's much to grieve over and only a general agreement that we must get on with it prevents us from giving ourselves over to sorrow. And to joy."

Alec Wilkinson

Chance

HE BELIEVED THAT love could be offered with an open hand. At a memorial for the poet Robert Fitzgerald, his oldest friend, he approached a man who had also been close to Fitzgerald. He knew the man slightly, and he said to him, "I feel that Robert has bequeathed us to each other." And in return got a blank look. In my mind's eye I can see Maxwell searching the man's face. Nothing, he thinks, and turns away. Maxwell had grown accustomed to indifference. His wife, Emily, felt that his deep humility came from having borne again and again the disappointment of his writing's not being as widely embraced as he had hoped it would be.

His attachment to his mother when he was a little boy was such that when she left the room, some intuition informed him, and if she wasn't back soon he would pick himself up and go looking for her. When she died, of influenza during the epidemic of 1918, while Maxwell was ten, he gave up any belief in a god who protected human happiness. No sensible person can fail to be astonished by creation, he thought, but the idea of an old man watching over individual lives, a being who judged, kept track, and intervened, who favored one person over another, a figure from a story—such a version had no meaning for him. His view was less sentimental—terrible things can happen at any moment, the universe is brute and mechanical, no agency protects the innocent, and it is unwise not to be prepared. Life continues even in the face of the unthinkable, one step after another, until eventually we reach the end. The point was to conduct oneself with dignity and courage, to be diligent in pursuit of the highest purposes, to find and nurture love, and to live while one has the chance. What happened at the end of life was a subject he never much cared to think about. An afternoon nap that goes on forever was how he imagined it.

As a young man he lived the life of a solitary. He was grateful for his job at *The New Yorker,* and he worked very hard, but what he feared would happen did happen, which was that reading and editing manuscripts, helping other writers, was so consuming that he had less and less time to think about stories. He lived in a small apartment off a courtyard in the West Village. The night a friend who lived in the building had brought him to see it, there were no lightbulbs, and he took the place because he liked the way that it felt in the dark. *The New Yorker* insisted he install a phone, but when it rang he usually waited for it to stop. The thought of another conversation in a day that had been full of them fatigued him. Another friend, noticing the geraniums on Maxwell's windowsill, said that he ought to look for a place in the country. A cottage that had been delivered to its acre of ground on a flatbed truck is what it turned out to be. The ride to the city on the train, along the Hudson River, took an hour. Three days a week Maxwell worked at the office. An elderly Frenchwoman kept house for him. Reading and writing all day did not strike her as a satisfactory occupation for a man.

He was in his thirties when he heard about Theodore Reik, a psychoanalyst who had studied with Freud. Five days a week, Maxwell occupied a couch in Reik's office. He felt as if he were living in a prison, he said—no wife, no family. After about a year of describing his child-hood, his dreams and their day remnants, he sat for two days at his typewriter, and what came out, he thought, was very strange. He was so angry at his parents for hav-ing another child—why hadn't they been satisfied with him?—that he had wished they would die. His father caught the flu also, but what happened to his mother made him, he felt—the child in him felt—a murderer. What do you do with a murderer? Put him in a jail cell. Reik eventually remarked that the cell wasn't locked.

Maxwell looked up the name in the phone book of a young woman who had come to his office a year earlier, hoping for a job in the poetry department. Emily Noyes.

She had dark eyes and black hair, which she wore piled on top of her head. Her features were delicately drawn, and she was tall and thin and moved gracefully. Her upright carriage came from having ridden a horse to school as a girl in Oregon. Maxwell felt that he had never seen any woman so beautiful, but at the time he did nothing about it. It was as if he were sleepwalking, he thought later. Her name wasn't in the book, but she had left it with the magazine's personnel department. She was teaching at a nursery school on the Upper East Side and had a room on the school's top floor. On their first date they went to a party given by one of his friends and talked only to each other. Then he walked her home, and as they sat on the school's steps, he asked her to marry him. He hadn't meant to, the words simply came out of his mouth. She said she didn't want to get married but that he could call her if he wanted to. He was thirty-five, and she was twenty-three. He closed up the house in the country and rented a ground floor apartment near the school in order to court her. In the Third Avenue saloons they often went to, she liked to drop coins into the jukebox and play the faux cowboy song "Don't Fence Me In." The party given for them the evening after they were married was held in a friend's apartment across the street from the apartment where, fifty-five years later, and eight days apart from each other, both of them died; she, first, at seventy-eight, from cancer, and he, at ninety-one, from old age.

She liked parties, and he didn't care for them much, unless he found someone he could talk to intimately.

While everyone else's eyes looked around the room for other opportunities, Maxwell usually sat beside someone companionable and heard how his or her family had escaped the Nazis and started life over in Paris, or how a young man or woman had grown up on a farm in the Midwest with an aunt who read Shakespeare out loud. He was fiercely interested in other people's lives, not because he meant to make use of what they told him—he never did, really, he wasn't that species of writer; his own life figured too prominently in his imagination—but because he felt that something about connecting to other people was sustaining.

She liked passionately held opinions, she liked a certain amount of posturing and display—especially if it was knowingly comic and essentially benign—and within reason she liked confession. Her own opinions were always subject to revision, not because she was without convictions, but because she believed in being receptive to a suggestion or a broadening remark. Whereas Maxwell replied to nearly everything someone said to him by offering something of himself, she encouraged others to reveal themselves but gave away very little concerning her own feelings, which amounted to a social sleight of hand. She was so attractive and her attention was so gratifying that a person often talked on and on, and got up from the dinner table feeling he had exchanged opinions with a beautiful and intelligent woman, when in fact most of the opinions had been his own. Because she responded warmly, though, and quickly, and because her eyes always held such radiance, one didn't usually notice. She would have loved, I think, to have been more carefree, but it wasn't in her nature. She worried too much in the middle of the night. Her behavior wasn't a question of bearing, it was a complicated form of timidity, something bred into her by a straitlaced growing up among prosperous people who were themselves not given to introspection and had a touch of melancholy. The house she was raised in was dark and full of heavy furniture and paintings and objects establishing a past. An indulgence is perhaps how they regarded self-dramatizing talk, a form of unhealthy attention, diverting one from a sturdy life. Perhaps they also considered it undignified, the habit of people whose hands couldn't keep still when they spoke. Her father was a businessman who had been raised in the Midwest and gone to Yale and afterward, influenced, I think, by Francis Parkman and his life lived outdoors, went to Oregon. For not much money he bought tracts of forestland and left them to mature. Thirty and forty years later, when he started to sell them, they had become valuable.

Maxwell felt that after he married his writing became more serious and psychologically acute. He dreamed one night that he flew to Paris in a box, and that when he saw how beautiful Paris was he flew back to get her. For his ninetieth birthday she gave him a small wooden box on which she had painted a lion resting at night in the branches of a tree. On the bottom of the box she wrote, "Each day I am as glad to see you as I am to see the sun rise in the morning and the moon cross the sky at night." He kept the box on his desk in the country. A few days before he died, he sent someone to get it, so that he could have it with him when his body was consigned to the flames.

. . .

MY FATHER BEQUEATHED me to him. He was introduced to Maxwell on a commuter-train platform by a neighbor, soon after Maxwell, in the late thirties, moved into the small house on the country road where my father and his first wife lived. My father, Kirk, was a magazine art director. He understood how machines worked, he knew carpentry, and he could fix anything he could put his hands on, whereas Maxwell could manage almost nothing for himself as a householder. "Dear Kirk," he wrote in a letter, "As I was riding through the woods beside you I was thinking Oh God if only just once it would be his car that broke down so I could be doing this for him. Over the years it has been so much." And on another occasion: "Last night, Emmy being in bed with a cold she picked up from some Portorican girl she was helping to learn to read in Harlem, I was sitting on the bed too, for company, reading the Times, after a busy day in Yorktown, and Kate"—the older of the Maxwells' daughters—"came calling, and what she was saying was that the pedals had fallen off the piano. It's Ann Heatherlin, I said to Emmy. She comes to practice on the piano in town, and as you may remember believes in good strong tones. But when I went and looked, it wasn't just the pedals. It was the whole shaft going down to the floor. And no Kirk, I said to myself bitterly. . . ."

In my father's workshop in the barn, Maxwell, with my father helping him, built a dollhouse for Kate at Christmas. When I read in *So Long, See You Tomorrow* the description of the two farmers repairing a piece of machinery that goes, "Wrenches and pliers pass back and forth between them with as much familiarity as if they owned their four hands in common," I think of Maxwell and my father building the dollhouse. They would ride to and from the train station in my father's jeep often without saying a word, each deeply content in the other's company. Another letter: "So strange. I walked into the Century Club this noon and saw the back of a head of black hair and thought it was you. This afternoon your letter came. Making me very homesick. For the way things were when you lived on the Road. The drives home. The workshop. And all of you." Because I am my father's son, I brought to my friendship with Maxwell many of the attributes my father did. Years later we often sat quietly with each other, on folding chairs beside a pond in the Wellfleet woods, in front of the fireplace in the house in the country, on the sofa in the living room of the Maxwell's apartment, a pot of tea or a bottle of champagne on the coffee table, the light from the windows growing darker until the lamps had to be switched on.

Another letter. It is winter, and in the yard there is a boy Maxwell has hired cutting wood for the stove in Mrs. Maxwell's studio; she was a painter. "Emmy is home, the boy is still splitting wood in what are now steady big cottony flakes of snow. How nice it was in the old days when we shared the weather together. The high point was surely when you left the road altogether"—my father had horses and a carriage sleigh—"and drove home over the fields. . . .

"It's now dark. I've just brought seven or eight big sheets of cardboard in from the studio. The cat is running like a streak across the snow with joie de vivre. I didn't want to come in either. I looked at the little lighted house and thought how I am more attached to it than to the apartment in town, more than to any other place on earth, and how I couldn't bear not to live here. The outside lights are all on, and there is an inch of what shines like artificial snow everywhere. So light, so full of glitter, and still falling out of the dark sky."

.   .   .

WRITING HIS FIRST novel, he worried that he was able to describe only the exterior of his character's lives, like icing on a cake, he said, and that he had no gift for penetrating their moods and thoughts. Prose that reproduced long sections of someone's thinking was never congenial to him. He was moved deeply by the little boy who was so close to his mother in Virginia Woolf's *To the Lighthouse,* but I never heard him say that he admired her efforts to depict the consciousness of her characters.

When he was younger he saw the short story as being something like a safe with a combination. The stories he wrote then tended to involve, he felt, a single situation that took place in front of the reader and in only one setting. The labor went into finding the combination that made the safe door swing open. It was a kind of story *The New Yorker* was partial to and, he felt, a reaction to the version of one that takes in a whole life. When he was older he was fond of Frank O'Connor's description of a story as presenting a moment of change in someone's life, an event of such significance that "the iron was bent, and anything that happens to that person afterwards, they never feel the same about again."

Actual happenings have their own pattern and drama, he believed, and if properly described had a substance that purely imagined events didn't have. He didn't mean that plain autobiographical writing—the account of a person's days, what he did and thought and whom he saw—was sufficient to engage a reader the way fiction could. Such writing needed to be arranged, analyzed, and to have a pattern found for it. Memoir worked best, he thought, when the writer's intention was, by means of candor, to lay open his life to the reader. Autobiographical fiction required that the writer hold things back, that he present only the most resonant details, perhaps reordered or divided among several characters. It needed to be done with restraint and objectivity. As if the writer were somehow above the action like a god, observing and recording, so that the reader felt that the events and feelings described were collective more than personal, that they formed an impression of human activity and feeling. He used always to say, "Pay attention," when I was on my way to any encounter that was emotionally fraught.

The stories of his older years—those in *Billie Dyer* and the ones toward the end of *All the Days and Nights*—and the novel *So Long, See You Tomorrow* have not their like in all American writing. The situations that gave rise to them—the unexpected passing of two boys in a school hallway, for example, and the guilt that one of them feels for having failed to acknowledge his friend; an old woman who resists an embrace—are substantially beyond the capabilities of most writers to dramatize. Once when he was an elderly man, we were riding in a taxi, and he said, "Whenever I write something now, I ask myself, 'Is this true?'"

Reading a book to review, he underlined the passages he liked. What he would have preferred doing, he once told me, is having the review consist of those passages, but in order to give the material form, he set about describing the narrative. He did not consider himself a critic, and the few observations he made tended to be about whether the writer wrote well or not. The reader could decide for himself whether he was drawn to the material.

He believed that he had no talent for thinking, for regarding a subject in the absence of feeling or the requirements of storytelling, for philosophy and abstractions. When he considered that a story or novel or review he was working on was finished, he read it backward, sentence by sentence, so that he could assess the writing without being distracted by the rhythm that builds up in a writer's mind when he knows what's coming.

My father tried to interest him in using the people

who lived on the road as subjects, but, except to describe in a story how my father's first wife tried one night to sew a ruffle around the edge of a bed my father was trying to sleep in, I don't think he ever did. My father would have liked to read stories in which he and his neighbors figured, but he also felt, I think, as people often do with writers, especially writers such as Maxwell who take so long to finish work, that he was helping his friend, who was probably stuck wondering what to write about.

Maxwell wrote slowly, that is, the typewriter keys fell slowly against the carriage. He wrote, it occurs to me, like the old man I knew him to be. Confident and without anxiety for where he was going, or how it would turn out, engaged by the appearance of one word after another on the page. Like the Japanese painter, possibly it's Hokusai, who signed his pictures "Old Man Crazy About Drawing." Seated at the typewriter, he put me in mind of a musician picking up his violin or his cello or placing his hands on the piano's keyboard to begin an engagement with something essential to his existence, knowing that it will be transporting and call on elements of the inner life—memories and dreams and images only otherwise half absorbed, if they arrived in consciousness at all. It was a behavior, an observance, he couldn't do without.

• • •

WHEN SOMEONE DIES, it becomes difficult to preserve a clear image of him or her. What remains after enough time has passed is a likeness influenced by what he meant to us and how ardently we recall him. To prevent myself as much as I can from losing sight of Maxwell, I keep on my desk a photograph of him that accompanied a memorial written by Daniel Menaker, one of the editors Maxwell trained to take his place when he left *The New Yorker,* in 1976. The essay appeared in *The New York Times Book Review.* The photograph is about the size of a large postcard. Maxwell is looking into the camera's lens. His eyes are slightly narrowed, and his lips are drawn. He is making no effort, that is, to smile. His expression is severe and slightly pained. What I like about the photograph is that he looks fierce, and in all the other photographs I have of him—from his childhood to when he was grown, including the portrait my father took of him for the dust jacket of *Time Will Darken It*—the principal impression is of gentleness, and while that was a signal part of Maxwell's character, it was by no means all. The fierceness is more prominent in his writing, in the fables, for example, which so often involve death, frequently arriving after much hardship and as an injustice.

About a year after the photograph appeared, I happened to find a copy of it. What the newspaper had cropped from it was Eudora Welty, standing beside Maxwell. I knew from the way Maxwell was dressed that the photograph had been taken at the annual ceremonial of the American Academy of Arts and Letters, because I had been there. Maxwell and Welty had left together. He had been her editor and she had dedicated one of her books to him and Emily. Maxwell and Welty rarely saw each other anymore because Welty didn't often come to New York. I watched them walking down the long promenade that leads to the street, two elderly figures, tipped sympathetically toward each other. Sometime after I turned away, they were stopped by the photographer. Maxwell's annoyance at the interruption is plain from the tightness of his lips, even though for another man the expression might be regarded as mild. I value the picture, because I knew the fierceness, and admired it.

He became aware as a young man that he might have sufficient talent to do work that would last and that what such a task required was a single-mindedness, a dedication to being an artist. Each artist, he believed, must wrestle with his talent the way Jacob wrestled all night with the angel and refused to let him go until the angel blessed him.

For forty years he worked seven days a week. Four days at writing and three days at the office. Requiring from his family a sacrifice, the cost of which he was aware of and insisted on. When I turn to him in my mind, the words he says are nearly always stern. If I am disconsolate, he says, "You must keep going. You have no other choice." He does not diminish the gravity of my concerns, but he does not indulge them, either. He does not do anything but encourage me to work harder, unless it is to give up if I feel the task is too great. "There are a lot of other ways to make a living," he used to say, if I was worried about money. Losing his mother he had described as the worst that could happen. He had gone on, and even as sympathetic as he was, he didn't see the need for indulgence. He was a product of the nineteenth century, and the country people in back of him. The preachers who believed that God was their refuge. The farmers with fields that needed their attention. The winters were cold, and in the spring there were fevers that bred in the swampy ground. Droughts arrived in the summer, along with locusts that could wipe out the harvest in a matter of days. Not to mention the women who died in childbirth, or the little boy or girl who had drunk from a tainted well. And for everyone enough work from the time they got up in the morning and lit lamps to see what they were doing to when they needed them again to read the Bible before going to bed. His mother had indulged him—her angel child, she called him—but after she died no one did until he was married, and perhaps he took an unconscious pleasure in telling other people that his example of life should also be theirs.

The other photograph I keep of him was taken in the year before he died by my wife at the house in the country. Maxwell is in his study. He is wearing his pajamas and bathrobe—he liked to go from the breakfast table to the typewriter and not shave or get dressed until he was done writing. He doesn't know that my wife is standing in the doorway. He is sitting at the typewriter, his hands are in his lap, and he is leaning forward, in an attitude of receptivity. It is there I like to think of him, the quiet figure, the old man, sitting at the desk, waiting for the words to come.

Charles Baxter

The Breath of Life

> I can never get enough of knowing
> about other people's lives.
> —*William Maxwell*

A CHARACTERISTIC POSTURE for him: leaning forward on a sofa, an oddly unreadable smile on his face (he is in his eighties), he asks you about your travels, your past, your *life*. "After I left Illinois," he says, "I was always a tourist, wherever I was." He is an old man and yet still quite curious about everything that people do. This curiosity is very disconcerting. Once I told him that as a Midwesterner, I didn't want to be taken as a provincial. "Oh, I do," he said, and laughed.

To resort to a parlor trick as he once did: if William Maxwell were an instrument of a symphony orchestra, what instrument would that be? In playing this trick himself for an essay included in *The Outermost Dream*, he once decided that V. S. Pritchett would be a bassoon, off to one side and not in the front rows. No great stretch of the imagination is required to think of William Maxwell himself, in a slightly higher register, as an oboe. Compared to the other woodwinds, the oboe is incapable of loudness. The brasses have to be silenced if you are going to hear it at all. Nor do you think of it for its power, if that is to be understood as sheer volume. The oboe is also incapable of hysteria—something the violins are good at. Still, of all the voices in the orchestra, the oboe is the one noted for perfect pitch and delicacy of tone. The other instruments can sometimes seem coarse in comparison. It has a companionable but somewhat lonely sound. Because of the requirements of breath control, it is very hard to play.

Even as I write out this analogy, I suspect that he would not have liked it. What worked for him will not work for others.

Although Maxwell never wrote a true autobiography, his life made its way into almost all of his books, particularly *So Long, See You Tomorrow*, his last novel, an unobtrusively perfect example of literary art of the highest humility and generosity. In it, the narrator does not at any point make an effort to disguise the fact that when he says "I," the "I" refers to the author himself. Nevertheless, the book is, among other things, a portrait gallery, including a depiction of its author, and I feel about *So Long, See You Tomorrow* the way Michael Ondaatje does, that it is "one of the great books of our age." One of the curiosities about this masterpiece, however, is that after setting himself on the stage of his own novel for a chapter or two, and having created his own self-portrait, William Maxwell then proceeds to take himself *off* that stage, to make himself invisible, although his presence as a storyteller remains and can be felt everywhere, like that oboe playing among the inner voices of the orchestra. In the removal of the narrator from his own story, Maxwell seemed, as a writer, to thrive: he was always more narratively and lyrically attuned to things taken away, to certain kinds of deprivations, than to things, or emotions, added on.

In saying that *So Long, See You Tomorrow* is a work of generosity, I mean that its author makes of himself a minor character so that the dramas of his childhood friend—Cletus Smith—and Cletus's father and mother, even his dog, and the neighbors, and the family members, and the people in the community, can be heard and seen and understood. His pleasure and his art are entirely given over to the lives of others in all their variety. Their lives stand in for his. A friend of mine once remarked that the book is unique in first-person accounts from Romanticism onward in that other people are not minor characters in the pageant of the author's life. Other novels with effaced narrators certainly do exist, but few with so personal a claim upon the narrator's own autobiography, including his traumas and tragedies, and perhaps none in which the author goes so far out of his way to suppress himself and to put others on the stage of his life, as if their lives were better examples of what he is demonstrating than his own.

This is not just a triumph of writerly technique and emotional balance; the displacement has something to do with the capaciousness—a word he liked—of his imaginative sympathies.

If *So Long, See You Tomorrow* presents an emotional and personal problem—being traumatically "stuck" in time because of a terrible loss, that of a parent—through its own example it then seems to present a solution: we become free of our own difficulties by imagining, in great and lively detail, the situations of others. Imagining the situation of others is a form of self-forgetting. It makes of the artist's task a permanent and even spiritual practice of negative capability. One learns how to lean forward on the sofa and to ask the guests about their lives. Perhaps this is a result of learning, as *So Long, See You Tomorrow* asserts, "that generosity might be the greatest pleasure there is."

The William Maxwell whom I knew slightly was not always so eager to talk about his own life. He could do so, vividly, but it always appeared to set him back, somehow. Whenever he did speak about the past, his face had traces of the boy he had once been, and, indeed, the presence of an almost childlike openness in some of his characteristic expressions gave him a passing quality of remarkably eerie sweetness. You could still see something youthful in the smiling face of the old man greeting you at the door. I never quite got over the unusual shadings that colored his expressions, and sometimes they made me uneasy. He baffled me, with his interest in my stories. All the old men I had accustomed myself to were reptilian in one way or another, conclusively closed up. They had taken in all the experience of the world they cared to take in, and now they considered it their job to offer or to inflict judgments, usually severe, on the world from which they would soon depart. He was so unlike that in both his writing and his person that encountering either one at first was a shock.

We once sat together in the living room of the Maxwells' apartment on East Eighty-sixth Street, talking mostly about travel. I had arrived in the early afternoon. He told me that someday I should go to the west coast of Ireland, where the clouds don't look like clouds anywhere else because they haven't passed over land. He himself had always wanted to go to Scotland, the land of his ancestors, but never had. There was always something else to see down south, he said. I told him that I had ambitions to see Russia. "One shouldn't go as a tourist to a country where people are suffering," he said, and it occurred to me that in fact he had never really liked to travel very much. He said, somewhat abruptly, that he had lived for fifty years in New York City but still was not a New Yorker.

As the afternoon went on, the light began to fail, and by evening the apartment was almost completely in darkness. We were still talking, even though we could hardly see each other. Maxwell did not seem to want to turn on any of the lights. He said he loved the darkening and the departure of the light from the room because it made the objects in it more lively, and when his wife came home, flipping on the switch as she came in, I saw his face again, rapt with attention. He told his wife that it was as if he and I had gone for a walk in the woods.

That quality of disconcerting openness, even of a mature and worldly spiritedness in an old man, with a notable admixture of melancholy, was always visibly present in our encounters. He seemed to know it. He inscribed one of his books to me, "From one good little boy to another." As a sentiment this is sweet and funny but also rather unnerving and sly and, of course, comically disingenuous. But it wasn't his somewhat tricky openness alone that I found so appealing and, at times, unworldly; it was his empathy, which seemed peculiarly enlarged, like an hypertrophied organ. Anyone might interest him. I have the shy person's trick of getting others to talk about themselves so that I don't have to make a conversational effort myself, but he was much better at that trick than I was and could effortlessly provoke stories from me or anyone else. In his letters, anecdotes about himself almost always turn into stories about other people. This, from a letter dated September 1997:

As Emmy does more and more I do less and less, as if only in this way can I hold down my end of the teeter-totter. Her brother, who lives outside Athens, is coming next week for a visit, the first in several years. So all the rugs in the house were carried away to be cleaned, and a man came to wax and polish the floors. A man (this will surely appeal to you) with no last name. Just call me Joe. He had stopped for directions at the vegetable stand in Yorktown and the woman there said Emmy had just left. So misled by the mailboxes, though there is a sign in our driveway, he waited two hours for her to come home. When he realized his mistake and walked in, Emmy said "Would you like a glass of water?" and he said "I never drink water." So she said "A cup of coffee and some toast?" This he accepted. He also fell in love with her and this led him, whenever I said anything, to reply "Just you relax." A thing I am only too given to doing anyway. If he has no last name he must have been illegitimate, I thought. And so he must have been, because he was brought up in foster homes, and much knocked about until he learned to defend himself. He did a very good job on the floors, in case you need to have yours polished, but left all the lamp cords unplugged, which I am afraid I hold against him. It is my belief that love is never unreciprocated. Anyway, Emmy talks about having him come back next year.

One paragraph. The narrator leaves the stage so that Joe, the aquaphobe, can appear and establish himself as a character and fall in love and even show jealousy, but somehow—and I can imagine how, because such curiosity was characteristic of him—the narrator has also found out about Joe's childhood, with all those foster homes and their attendant difficulties, and he has in addition found out about his acquisition of pugilistic skills. The subject of this person's upbringing gets mixed up with Joe's having fallen in love with the letter writer's wife, as if *So Long, See You Tomorrow* is being replayed briefly, in miniature, for anecdotal comedy. There is a curious selflessness to this, to the way Joe is permitted to take the stage and stay there. And then, too, there is the line "It is my belief that love is never unreciprocated."

. . .

It is a shock to read *So Long, See You Tomorrow* after reading other novels of the Midwest set in its time and approximate place. *Main Street, Winesburg, Ohio,* Cather's *A Lost Lady,* for example—all of them press their various provincials into service as either oversensitive outsiders or loutish boosters. In the case of *Main Street,* the cartooning has a way of backfiring: Dr. Will Kennicott, the oafish country doctor, comes to seem more interesting and complicated than his "cultured" wife, Carol, the ostensible heroine of the novel, who believes in salvation through upper-middlebrow art. In this book it is as if attending the plays of Ibsen and listening to Rachmaninoff solve the entire problem of the Midwest. Lewis's novels—as has been often noted—are marred by their author's apparent belief that most people are neither complex nor interesting except by virtue of their routines, and they therefore deserve to be lampooned, so that they may become comical or at least entertaining in a superficial way. The writer does not see other people as being particularly complex, and so in his books they are not. But the habit of satire and cartooning is almost wholly absent from Maxwell's novels, except for the first one, which he never wanted reprinted. He appeared to believe that every character, good or bad, deserves to be treated with respect.

This is a Chekhovian assumption, that every life contains its own nearly unfathomable mystery. Even those who may seem simple on the surface are complex in the means by which they navigate from day to day. No one's struggles with life are without interest. Maxwell liked to quote Ortega, to the effect that life was in itself and forever shipwreck. Therefore, to find any life interesting, you would merely have to look at it long enough.

And that is why I want to talk about the dog.

· · ·

IN *So Long, See You Tomorrow* there is a dog named Trixie who belongs to Cletus Smith, the murderer's son. The dog meets the boy every afternoon when the boy comes home from school. The dog is announced in the novel as an "invention" by the book's author, but most readers probably forget that particular announcement or pay no attention to it. Anyway, the dog leads the boy from the main road up the driveway every school day, "trot[ting] on ahead importantly."

Early on in the novel (we are still in Chapter 5), we learn about the dog's life, and Cletus's life, by means of a series of inventories accomplished with great artfulness. The reader is given lists of objects with which the dog is familiar and then, when Cletus enters the house, a list of the objects in the kitchen from which the boy takes comfort. Steam on the windows. Zinc surfaces. The embossed calendar. The cracked oilcloth on the kitchen table. The list goes on and on, but it does not become wearisome because something tells the reader that all this is fragile and will soon disappear. This boy inhabits this particular world, a voice seems to say, and it will soon be gone. We have already been given a similar inventory of the narrator's own surroundings, just before and immediately after his mother's death.

Love appears to be reciprocated everywhere in the setting through which Cletus travels, except, crucially, between his parents. When he goes to the pasture fence, "an old white workhorse comes, expecting a lump of sugar and possibly hoping to be loved. Anyway, Cletus loves him." At night the sky is powdered with stars.

We are not permitted to believe that these scenes are idyllic because we have already been informed of several disasters that will shortly occur. The narrator's mother will die in the flu epidemic of 1918. Cletus's father will murder a neighboring farmer, once his best friend, and then will commit suicide. The narrator will be friendless and inconsolable for a long period of time, and every particle of what both Cletus and the narrator have loved will be taken away. Their worlds will be destroyed, and, being children and mostly wordless, they will have no sentences for these unaccountable losses, and they will not be given any. They will be inarticulate, as their parents are, either by choice or disposition. In *So Long, See You Tomorrow* the words that people need to speak in order to save their own or others' lives are almost never spoken, simply because they can't be. Unspoken words are at the center of this book. They constitute its great puzzle. They are more of a mystery than a murder, whose logic is relatively simple.

Americans often regard being laconic as a virtue. The strong silent man has been a traditional icon in our culture. But in Maxwell's novel a refusal or inability to speak brings on heartsickness, the misery of the unsaid. I once started an inventory of the instances in *So Long, See You Tomorrow* of characters' not saying or not telling what should be articulated. I gave up because the list was getting too long. The repetitions seemed so obvious that there was no point in cataloging them. And they all had to do with love: love offered, but not accepted; love or friendship that goes begging or unacknowledged; love that has been removed from the scene of action; or suffering so intense that it has moved beyond words entirely and can't be spoken of.

In addition to using the technique of the dramatic inventory, objects given and then taken away, and notations of dramatic air pockets of dead silence, Maxwell tended to build his narrative accumulations by creating correspondences everywhere. To begin with, there are corresponding dramatic images: a half-built house with walls you can walk through rhymes with Giacometti's *The Palace at Four A.M.* which in turn rhymes with a fence that a child can somehow penetrate. These, in turn, are set in relation to correspondences between the narrator's father (all the sentences he does not say) and Cletus's father (all the things he *cannot* say). Maxwell is very careful to notice the distinctions of class between the characters and the economic differentiation between the middle class, where an inventory is characteristic of business practices and has a touch of vaingloriousness, and tenant farmers, whose inventories are a matter of sheer survival. What a person or an animal needs to get by is also at the heart of this novel; the struggle for survival on earth constitutes a central dramatic situation.

What happens to one set of characters in this novel, therefore, is likely to happen to another set of characters (including the animals) in slightly different form, through a series of correspondences. The problem of being unable to say what you mean, or for that matter to say anything at all, is so pervasive that the animals and the people in this setting are not separated greatly in form or character. They simply arrive, innocent creatures, man and beast, on different points of the continuum; they echo each other. The humans behave at times like animals, with inarticulate violence (no one objects to this as a dramatic device), and the animals sometimes behave with an almost human understanding whenever the worlds they are accustomed to are suddenly dismantled. This is what everybody remembers about the novel: the behavior of the dog when the world she has grown used to is taken away. She is mystified. The dog appears to think about her losses, and her thoughts are given to us in the book.

From the very start, the dog caused the book's first readers trouble. In an obituary piece on Maxwell in *The New York Times*, Daniel Menaker remembers that Maxwell's editor at *The New Yorker*, Roger Angell, "and others of us in the department thought the dog was a mistake." One hears here the confidence of a collective taste. Menaker goes on to observe that Roger Angell encouraged Maxwell "to put the thinking dog to sleep." Note the lighthearted tone. But Maxwell wasn't having any of it, the lightheartedness or the objections. In a letter to Angell now stored in the William Maxwell Collection at the University of Illinois at Urbana-Champaign, Maxwell refused to back down:

> I'm sorry Shawn [then editor of *The New Yorker*] is allergic to that dog. It is based on our Daisy, whose emotions and thoughts were transparent. I am not silly over dogs in general, and as it now stands I don't think there is a single detail that I do not believe to be easily possible. In any case, I have explicitly stated, part I, galley 41, that the dog is an invention. I have also said, in the paragraph above, that if any part of the following mixture of truth and fiction strikes the reader as unconvincing, he has my permission to disregard it. I think most readers will either believe in the dog or take it to be a fictional device—which it is. I have done Cletus through the dog's eyes, hoping that some of the love will wear off on the reader. Any piece of writing involves choices, and I chose to do it this way is what it amounts to, and it is now too late to chose [*sic*] some other way.

The dog as fictional device: as the earlier worlds of the book are taken apart through death or violence, the dog observes much of it and becomes a vessel of pure feeling. The dog stays in *So Long, See You Tomorrow* so that finally she can express the core emotion of the book, deprivation. She begins howling, is what it amounts to. "They" have taken the other animals away, and they have taken her boy away, and they have taken her food away, and they have also taken away her purpose for being on the farm, and after waiting for a long time, trying not to worry, she can't help herself: "Eventually, in spite of her, the howls broke out. Sitting on her haunches, with her muzzle raised to the night sky, she howled and howled."

Anyone reading *So Long, See You Tomorrow* with any alertness will notice that the dog's situation is similar to the narrator's. They have both had the love to which they had become accustomed removed. So, too, with Cletus: what he has loved has been taken away. Clarence Smith has been deprived of his wife's love, with the result that "He had no idea how long some of his silences were." The correspondences are everywhere. The narrator's father will not speak of his deceased wife, the narrator's mother, and Lloyd Wilson cannot or will not speak of his love in his letters to Cletus's mother, who imagines the love there anyway, between the lines. Somewhere underneath all this reticence and silence, however, something starts to howl, to raise its voice in protest and agony. That "something" is the dog, who can't help herself.

Readers and critics and editors who take for granted all the resources of articulate speech might well be baffled by such a story. Why, in the depth of various despairs, should anyone be unable to speak plainly? And why would anyone assume that a dog—a mere farm dog, at that—could possibly know what is going on around her, and give expression to it? You would almost have to be a provincial to believe such things.

There is one other passage in *So Long, See You Tomorrow* that everyone remembers. In the novel's grand coda, in which the various themes are set down next to one another in a kind of intricate counterpoint, a series of echo effects, the narrator recounts an analytic session during which, speaking of his mother's death, he meant to say, "I couldn't bear it," and instead says, "I can't bear it." This is followed by a "flood of tears such as I hadn't ever known before." The narrator leaves the analyst's office and walks down Sixth Avenue to his own office, still weeping. The pain that was supposed to die out hasn't. In New York, he observes, "one can weep on the sidewalk in perfect privacy."

What I want to say about these passages may appear to be strange and paradoxical. Maxwell, as everyone knows, was a fiction editor at *The New Yorker* for many years. In that capacity he was something of a wizard in recognizing what he liked to call "the breath of life" in other writers' fiction. He knew—there is no other way to say this—everything there was to know about sentences employed for storytelling. Nothing about fictional constructions seemed to escape him. Reading the correspondence between Maxwell and Frank O'Connor merely corroborates this observation. And yet there is a difference between knowing everything there is to know about sentences and *believing* in sentences, that is, sentences as a cure for emotions that might lie beyond them. Maxwell believed that in moments of extremity, sentences might very well fail you. He wished this situation were otherwise, but he knew perfectly well it was not. In *So Long, See You Tomorrow* all the major characters grow silent much of the time. Sometimes all they, and we, can do is weep, or howl. Later, after the fact, we may be able to piece together, if we have the patience and care of a watchmaker, the circumstances that led to the failure of words. Words will take us right to the edge of wordlessness; they will point to how the failure happens. We must say what is in our hearts if we can. But when we can't, words can point to the howling, but they cannot quite howl themselves.

Maxwell was a writer who lived in New York for fifty years but did not believe, or so he said to me, that he was a New Yorker. A *New Yorker* editor who claimed not to be a New Yorker! He did not mind, he said, being taken as a provincial. Again, this was somewhat disingenuous, because at his dinner table you were likely to be asked which biography of John Keats was your favorite, or which particular recorded performance of the Schubert piano trios caught the essence of the music most clearly. All the same, in his belief that all the blessed signs and wonders of civilized life are thin constructions over brute behavior and wretchedness, he lacked a certain urbane nonchalance. He remained a doubter at the feast. In his novels and many of his stories we are led by art and perfectly articulated sentences to a scene of cruelty, or loss, or misbehavior so extreme that one is silenced. The scenes arise not out of a struggle for power but from an effort to hold on, sometimes desperately, to what is loved and likely to be lost.

Maxwell, like any writer, had his limitations, and said so. He noted in interviews that his canvases might have been larger, that he might have, given different circumstances, had more varieties of subject to write about. He felt, and others sometimes noticed, that he occasionally repeated himself. Other flaws were noted. Some were put off by Maxwell's surfeit of feelings and, in person, the unexpected fits of weeping. And yet: Maxwell's persistence in his themes and subjects, along with his habit of undefended emotion, and what seemed to be an extraordinary imaginative generosity, led to his great virtue: his steady refusal to be glib. If he said it, it seemed true. At *The New Yorker*, he remained someone from Illinois who had been scarred forever by something that had happened to him there and who therefore believed in the limits of what might be said, the limits of art, the limits of language itself, although he believed, at all times, in the importance of speaking your heart as clearly as you could. In this respect he was like a mole planted in the CIA. Unlike the mole, however, he always endeavored to tell the truth. He would never say or write a sentence merely to create an effect.

This refusal kept him safely off the boulevards where the flaneurs were free to operate. It may also have kept him off the lists of best-selling fiction. But the refusal to be facile, combined with the unusual warmth of his storytelling, and his curious democratic principles (thinking dogs), and the beauty and economy of his sentences, and the artistry of his storytelling, created a phenomenon of sorts: he became, during his lifetime, beloved. That is, both the writing and the man aroused unusual affection. To an extent that is quite unusual in this country, his books were *loved,* rather than just admired. It was strange. In a culture not noted for its literary heroes or its civility, he himself was beloved by many, several of whom (I include myself) were bewildered by their own feelings about him but who had those feelings anyway.

Near the end of *So Long, See You Tomorrow* you can see all the threads of the novel being braided together. The narrator appears for the last time in his analyst's office. Cletus Smith reappears in the Chicago high school where, once again, he meets the narrator and is, once again, not acknowledged. The walls between the rooms are porous. "What is done can be undone. It is there that I find Cletus Smith." The past is not over but reappears in a series of reincarnations. The dead, however, stay dead, though their images do sometimes come back. And then the novel ends in a final paragraph built out of conjectures. But they are not about the narrator's life, except parenthetically. Once again the narrator has given his life over to someone else. The conjectures are all about Cletus Smith, who carries the burden of the narrator's feelings and who is the necessary object of the narrator's imaginings.

The sentences ask whether a series of terrible events might eventually come to be (to Cletus, a murderer's son, a boy raised on a farm) "less real, more like something he dreamed, so that instead of being stuck there he could go on and by the grace of God lead his own life, undestroyed by what was not his doing." In an audio recording of these sentences, Maxwell's voice does not quaver when he comes to this paragraph but instead sounds steely, as if he knew perfectly well how easy it might be to find oneself destroyed by events. One false step—not your own but someone else's and maybe just an accidental step—gradually causes the tearing apart of your world. The imaginative pressure on the sentences is considerable and all but invisible. You can read Maxwell's sentences over and over again and not notice that he has invented a word to serve his purposes. The word is so unobtrusive that you may not perceive that the entire novel has been built around it. The word I am referring to is "undestroyed." Of course, everybody knows what this word stands for, but it is doubtful that the word has previously been employed for literary purposes; it's a very odd word, and I would challenge anyone to find it in another book. Take it out of the sentence it appears in and it immediately looks peculiar. What does "undestroyed" mean, what does it refer to? Perhaps to the return of a prior condition, a state in which the blows have lost their power to hurt or to harm.

What is done can be undone. Perhaps, if one is lucky, one will be *undestroyed.* Except that, as the book makes mercilessly clear, the neighbor *has* been murdered and mutilated, the father *has* committed this crime and then committed suicide, the dog *has* indeed been destroyed, the mother *has* died from influenza, and no one has said the right words at the right time to undo any of it. What is done can be undone, but *only in this book,* only by means of art. Only in this novel does the word "destroy" have a suffix to put it in the past *and* a prefix to negate it. To hold the destruction, on both sides, in suspension.

.   .   .

IN HIS EMOTIONAL vulnerability, his openness, his combination of learned civility with a certain unforced spontaneity, Maxwell resembled (for me) another writer from the Midwest who was also loved by many readers, James Wright. Both writers seemed to be unusually unprotected, or to lack some layer of armor, and to have therefore exposed themselves, quite willingly, to the accusation that their writings could be naive or senti-mental. At the same time, their mastery of the formal techniques of their art was total—above reproach. And like Maxwell, though at times more violently, James Wright was a sworn enemy of glibness. He was known at cocktail parties to rise in anger at the spectacle of some boulevardier self-delightedly spreading bons mots and to shout, "You are the scum of the earth!"

I never heard Maxwell raise his voice, but I knew he had considerable anger in him, and a fair quantity of steel and savvy and self-interest. He was a survivor, after all. But in making a case for him as an exceptional writer and human being, a person who seemed to inspire love in others, I have to return, finally, to his generosity and openness as a writer and friend. At the end of *So Long, See You Tomorrow* you feel that you have been given considerably more of what is precious to its author than is often the case in novels of many hundreds of pages. What Maxwell has loved, he gives away in that book. "If Schubert were ever to come back to Earth," he once said to me, "he could come into my house and take anything."

At his memorial service I turned to a friend and told her this story regarding Schubert's return. She was not particularly surprised or impressed. "He would give anything to anybody," she said. No; I doubted that, then and now. He would *not* give anything to anybody, because he was not a fool and because he was not like that. But in the books, yes, always.

Benjamin Cheever

Something to Read
When He Dies

WILLIAM MAXWELL had trouble believing in God. I believe in God. I had trouble believing in William Maxwell.

I still don't think Bill is dead. But then I never had any real confidence that he was alive or, rather—to use the sort of qualifying clause that Bill was not afraid of— I didn't believe that such a man could exist.

Bill and I corresponded regularly, and had tea every couple of months. This went on for twenty years, and yet I never headed off to see Bill without expecting to find somebody else. It's worse than that. I never opened a letter, without expecting it to have been written by a different man.

At tea, I'd watch his face closely in order to catch the first stages of the transformation. You know when Lon Chaney looks at his hand and sees the thick black hair sprouting? I was checking for that. Or when the man living in the Alpine village goes out at night to kill the werewolf and tells his tiny son, "If I come back after the clock has struck, then bar the door."

I suppose you could say that I was expecting Bill to morph into my father, and there's some truth here. Bill and I were closest after my father had died. I missed my father, and what I missed most acutely in my father was the occasional brilliant flash of rage, which used to illuminate my world.

So I was looking for lightning, but to reduce my friendship with Bill to its connection with my father would be the same as to conclude that a man who owns an umbrella must be a meteorologist.

Still, that's where it begins. Bill was my father's editor at *The New Yorker,* and they got along remarkably well when you consider that Bill was my father's editor at *The New Yorker.* That's a big consider. If you're a writer and attempting to support a family, and you submit a story to your editor and he turns it down . . . or—in the parlance of *The New Yorker*—he doesn't think it quite works . . . well that's a blow to the friendship. And it might be a mortal blow, if the man who had given it had not been an editor . . . if the man who received it had not been a writer attempting to support a family.

Bill appeared at our house from time to time when I

was a child and even then I saw him as a contradiction. He seemed the gentlest of men, and yet I knew that he could wield a terrible power.

My father wrote with such confidence and conviction that many of his most devoted readers think he must have ruled the world. My father did not rule the world. He did, however, rule the world of his imagination, which is where we, his children, got our start. Bill was referenced in this world and not always in a flattering light. Often and often, I heard about how this full-grown man had come upon a dead pigeon and then burst into tears. Always a pigeon; never a sparrow.

In a letter to the novelist Allan Gurganas, from whom Bill had recently purchased a story, my father wrote, "Bill, as you must have gathered, is terribly fastidious. He once called to say that he was coming to tea. Mary went wild and cleaned, waxed, arranged flowers, etc. When he arrived everything seemed in order. Mary poured the tea. The scene was a triumph of decorum until Harmon, an enormous cat, entered the room, carrying a dead goldfish. It seemed to be our relationship in a nutshell."

Cheever legend had it that when both men were young and living in Manhattan, Bill had tried to kill my father by coming up from behind at a cocktail party and knocking him out of a window. In an interview with the BBC Bill recollected that he had been on the street below and that my father was pushed by a man from Minneapolis, who hadn't seen the iron spiked fence on which he was very nearly impaled. "John went to his grave believing I had pushed him out of the window intending to murder him," Bill said.

I relish this story, because it mixes professional and personal passions. Both men were beautiful when young. I don't know if they were attracted to one another. If there was an attraction it faded. What lasted was the shared appetite for excellent prose. They didn't always agree, but they always cared. The stakes were high. The stakes were life and death.

I suppose both men were ambitious, and yet they were not ambitious in the way the term is understood today. They were ambitious for themselves, but also for literature. My father liked to say that writing was not a competitive sport. Appearing onstage with a cane and made bald by chemotherapy, he told the audience at the American Book Awards that literature was the only record of man's attempt to be illustrious.

Literature was Bill's religion. Every argument I made for the existence of God, he'd counter with an example of something splendid that I should read. Sometimes he'd put his hand right on the book and send it home with me. Other times, he couldn't find the piece he was talking about it, and in these cases the wonder of the accomplishment seemed to be magnified by the elusiveness of the text. I remember him growing ecstatic one afternoon with his recollection of Tolstoy's "Master and Man."

I didn't always read what was suggested, but this story I found. It would be best here to insert the entire story, but I can't do that without exceeding my word count, so please excuse me for pulling two brief quotes to make a point. Having covered his despised servant with his own body when both men are lost in a blizzard, the master, Vasili Andreevich, hears a voice: " 'I'm coming! Coming!' he responded gladly, and his whole being was filled with joyful emotion. He felt himself free and that nothing could hold him back any longer.

"After that Vasili Andreevich neither saw, heard nor felt anything more in this world."

Clearer evocation of faith would be difficult to find, or phrase. The story ends when the servant himself dies twenty years after the blizzard in which his master—in a dramatically uncharacteristic act of selflessness—saved his life: "He also took leave of his son and grandchildren, and died sincerely glad that he was relieving his son and daughter-in-law of the burden of having to feed him, and that he was now really passing from this life of which he was weary into that other life which every year and every hour grew clearer and more desirable to him. Whether he is better or worse off there where he awoke after his death, whether he was disappointed or found there what he expected, we shall all soon learn."

Bill enjoyed his own writing enormously, but he delighted in the work of others. He pointed me toward Alec Wilkinson's nonfiction, Bernard Shaw's letters, Annabel Davis-Goff's memoir, Elizabeth Bowen's *The House in Paris*. They were all worth reading and this was all that mattered. Ranking them in order of achievement was not the sort of chore he had any interest in.

Of course there were books Bill disdained. This had almost as much to do with the motives of the writer, as with the result. Bill displayed very little interest in commercial success. Those who composed with a canny and calculating eye were distrusted. Bill echoed E. B. White who wrote once that "A writer who questions the capacity of the person at the other end of the line is not a writer at all, merely a schemer."

"Writing should be as natural as breathing," Bill told me, "and—whenever possible—as unselfconscious." Bill felt that everyone could write.

This seemed wonderfully generous to me. I suspected that it was too generous. Too Christian even. Can we all really be saved?

When I began to work on my father's letters, I went to Bill's apartment on Eighty-sixth Street for tea and to collect the letters he had kept. I wasn't certain that I was up to the task. "I'm not a scholar," I said. Bill paused, considered. "I hate scholars," he said.

From then on, I began to visit regularly. We shared more than a love of books and a mutual admiration for my father's prose. I remember telling him how delighted I was when I first came upon the word "masochist." "I thought if they had a word for it, then it couldn't be all that unusual."

Bill and I and Emmy and my wife Janet used to go to dinner once or twice a year, and I remember enjoying these events, but also contrasting them with the ethereal atmosphere of our solitary teas. Like church, Bill's house and apartment were both quiet. Visiting, I was inclined to whisper. He and Emmy were surrounded with totemic objects—her glorious paintings, worn copies of the works of the men and women he most admired. Bill moved slowly. If you asked him a question, he took it seriously, took his time before he answered. Our conversations sometimes verged on the ceremonial. He was as precise with his silences as he was with his words.

I came to rely on his judgment. I felt that the book of letters should acknowledge my father's bisexuality. If I was going to print love letters to women, I thought I should also print love letters to men. I suspected that I would be attacked for this, as my sister had been attacked for her memoir, *Home Before Dark*. And yet I didn't see how anyone could hope to understand my father without coming to grips with this side of his character. Plus, I thought with some bitterness that if I had had to acknowledge this truth, then others, a lot farther from ground zero, could jolly well come aboard.

But then I've always had difficulty distinguishing between lying and manners. Bill had excellent manners, and so I wanted to know what he thought. He told me to go ahead.

"Voltaire said (and I think he was right)," Bill told the BBC later, "that we owe nothing to the dead but the truth. If people think less well of Cheever because of the things his son and daughter have published since his death, then it means to me that they wanted Cheever to be their idea of him, at the expense of knowing who and what he really was. Would we like or prefer to know less about Flaubert (who was quite as shocking in his diaries, if not more, than Cheever) in order to find him less upsetting? It is too silly."

"But it would be inaccurate," I said at one point, "to see my father as an unhappy man."

"It would not only be inaccurate," said Bill, "it would be impertinent." This was said without judgment, without even a hint of condemnation.

After I'd published the first book, I went to Bill and told him, my voice creaking, "I always wished, I always imagined, that someday my father would take me aside and teach me how to write."

"Well," said Bill. "Obviously, he has taught you how to write."

Hypercritical men, my father had taught me, were often cruel, to themselves and then to others. Could a man as kind as Bill also write with precision?

After we'd had tea, I'd get out one of his books and move cautiously about in it tapping the foundations for sounds of rot. Bill's prose has a long fuse. He builds slowly toward his effects. He hypnotizes his readers. You have to sit down with the book. You can't wade in up to your ankles like a blue heron and pluck out colorful little fish. He didn't write for Bazooka.

And yet, I never go very far in my reading without coming upon something vital and resonant. This, for instance, from *The Folded Leaf*: "The truth is that Lymie had never wanted to die, never at any time. The truth is nothing like as simple or as straightforward a thing as Lymie believed it to be. It masquerades in inversions and paradoxes, is easier to get at in a lie than in an honest statement. If pursued, the truth withdraws, puts on one false face after another, and finally goes underground, where it can only be got at in the complex, agonizing absurdity of dreams."

Or this from *Ancestors*: " 'I was living in a rooming house on Lexington Avenue and I had dinner with somebody from the office one night who said there was a vacant apartment in the building where he lived, so I went home with him, and the door was unlocked but there weren't any light bulbs, and I took it because I liked the way it felt in the dark. The rent is thirty-five dollars a month. You go past an iron gate into a courtyard with gas streetlamps. It was built during the Civil War, I think. Anyway, it's very old. And my apartment is on the third floor, looking out on a different courtyard with trees in it. Ailanthus trees. I like having something green to look at. Technically it's a room and a half. The half is a bedroom just big enough for a single bed, and I never sleep there because it's too like lying in a coffin. I sleep on a studio couch in the living room. The fireplace works. And once when I had done something I was terribly ashamed of, I went and put my forehead on the mantelpiece. It was just the right height.' "

So then I'd pop out on the other side of my unbelief and conclude that the kindness must be faked. Bill's affection must be faked. I'd write long letters seeking to wake the monster. To which he'd would respond:

Dear Ben,

You didn't stay too long, or make us late for dinner, or bore either of us, or cause any problems.

Or else:

Dear Ben:

What do you mean you're not funny? You're terribly funny.

Sometimes he'd even enclose a copy of a letter I'd sent to him as proof—he thought—of my abilities.

When I got one of these letters, I'd read it, put it back in its envelope and leave it to mark a spot in *The New Scofield Study Bible* or in *Benét's Reader's Encyclopedia*. Then, with any luck, I'd be able to come upon it again, quite by accident, and again I'd have my spirits raised.

Going now through a shoe box full of his letters and reaching into an envelope, I can't entirely escape the sensations of a little boy unwrapping a Christmas gift. It is easy to summon my father's old friend. He's looking for a treasured volume in the shelves that line the living room of his apartment. The walls are bathed with the last amber rays of what my father liked to call a river light. I see the fine, long, intelligent face. I hear measured breathing.

I've read most of Bill's writing, but not all of it. Sometimes I'll go back again and read something that I particularly enjoyed, but there are other books I've never broached. I'm saving them. I want something fresh and lively to read when he dies.

Shirley Hazzard

William Maxwell

In his eighties, William Maxwell told me, "I love being old." By then, Bill Maxwell had recurrent and sometimes serious bodily infirmities. His mind and spirit were perhaps at their ripest power and would remain so until his death, ten years later. Those years were blessed by his long and luminous marriage, by his love for his daughters, and by the birth of the grandson who so resembles him. Bill had long since been delivered from the burden of what had been to him, in earlier years, an incapacitating sensibility: the "difficulty of being" no longer held terrors; "Fear no more the heat of the sun." His advancing age was as yet no hindrance to new work, and was enriched by the close affection of friends and by the homage to his art and his character that, having come rather late in his writing life, was now overwhelming and worldwide.

William Maxwell's life, considered in outline, might seem quite divided. The childhood that he would look back on as enchanted in its security—of place and family life, and through his mother's tender love—had been sundered by excruciating loss and loneliness. His mother's early death haunted Maxwell's life and work, and played its powerful part in the making of a writer. Incredulity at that severance stayed with him to the end. He understood this very well: few men have understood themselves as deeply.

The transformation came through his chance meeting with Emily Noyes, and the development of their great, reciprocated love. The ground, however, had been in some ways prepared. There had already been a measure of rescue by language and literature, and by the discovery and exercise of talent: the painful rescue, as it often is, through self-expression, intelligence, imagination. Maxwell was not drawn to intellectualism. His gift lay in acute humane perception. His response to existence derived from vulnerability and from intensity of observation.

I don't seek, here, to "explain"; only to give impressions from an unclouded friendship of forty years. Bill Maxwell took my first writing from the slush pile of *The New Yorker* and published it. He then took the trouble to get in touch with me and asked me to come to see him at the magazine. His encouragement, his genius, and his generosity transformed my own existence—as they did the lives of other writers. When I met Francis Steegmuller, who became my husband, we found an immediate, talismanic bond in the discovery of shared friendship with the Maxwells. Francis Steegmuller had known Bill since their youth at the infant *New Yorker.*

The human encounter came always fresh to Maxwell. Singularity was intrinsic to his own nature and to his sense of other lives. He knew the world deeply, yet remained accessible to it, detached from the contemporary trend toward exposition and pronouncement. That he kept faith with the wound of his early knowledge helped him, I think, to become a happy man.

Alec Wilkinson has splendidly written that Maxwell, in conversation, considered the effect of his words on the person whom he addressed. This does not, I feel, suggest that Bill's responses were always acquiescent or uncritical—although indeed he was an embodiment of the sympathy and tolerance apparent in his very being. But disagreement was, with him, a reasoned matter: he was free of mere self-assertion. His views were large, but firm. Inauthenticity, calculation, underhandedness drew his testy dismissal. He would not praise writing that he found spurious, no matter how expertly presented.

I believe that Bill would have felt the validity of Graham Greene's remark that the novelist conserves a splinter of ice in the heart. He had the writer's need to defend the secret writing mind, where objectivity and syllables must alike be nurtured and weighed, and the deeper, unshared self explored and plundered for treasure.

The rescue that came to him in the middle of his life was favored also by the climate of *The New Yorker,* where Bill worked for forty years—with Harold Ross, the first editor, and at length with William Shawn. Both Ross and Shawn, in contrasting ways, were oddballs, and had a feeling for the talents of fellow oddballs. Ross had a reputation for cryptic humor, and a brash aptitude for creativity. Shawn, unprecedented and unreproducible, remains an irreducible figure in the cultural story of New York or any other city. In late years, Maxwell had his differences with Shawn. But the decades during which they worked closely and cordially together were a period of rich literary achievement that, I imagine, no prominent magazine will ever enjoy again. To have been associated with *The New Yorker* during that period was revelatory, fascinating, and fun. Maxwell brought his generosity of spirit to the work of others. His feeling for one's work was never, in my experience, intrusive. He respected the creative intention. He loved fiction, and loved the stories of our lives. His relations, of trust and tact, with authors are finely attested in his published correspondence with Frank O'Connor.

Maxwell paid tribute, in conversation and interviews, to another phase of his emergence from the griefs of his early years, saying that the psychoanalyst Theodor Reik had given him "a life." Two of Bill's comments on Reik's interventions seem at variance with Maxwell's temperament, although he relates them in a favorable sense. Reik felt that Maxwell should more actively seek recognition in his writing career, should be more ambitious for winning prizes. Yet it is precisely Bill's characteristic restraint in these matters that, viewed from the perspective of his long life, appears to have deepened the wide recognition that eventually came to him and, in retrospect, even seems to have mysteriously compelled it. Maxwell's instinct in this was appropriate and true. Bill also cites, again seemingly with approval, Reik's prohibition: "No remorse, no remorse." In both these correctives, it is hard to recognize Maxwell, and it seems possible that the analyst was seeking to reverse an excess of diffidence or self-accusation. A remorseless person is not an attractive phenomenon. Through responsibility and regret we come to know ourselves, and Maxwell's personality and writings attest these qualities in their consideration for the sensibilities of others. Bill told me that he had, in latter middle age, written to each of several persons whom he thought he had wronged in earlier years: an exercise in apology and—one would have thought—remorse. On this theme, one thinks of Yeats—

> Things said or done long years ago,
> Or things I did not do or say
> . . . .
> Weigh me down, and not a day
> But something is recalled,
> My conscience or my vanity appalled.

In his last extraordinary year of life, while Emily Maxwell was slowly dying with a grace, a philosophy, and, I would say, a beauty that remain indescribable, Bill

Maxwell reread *War and Peace*. His solace and pleasure in the book were an event in those rooms. He said, "It is so comforting." We rejoiced together over certain scenes, not "discussing" or dissecting them but paying, simply, the tribute of our delight. He would speak of these episodes shedding his silent tears—not in grief but for the grandeur of common humanity. Bill was steadily eating less, and when the book became too heavy for him to hold, a friend—Annabel Davis-Goff—came each afternoon and read it to him.

Five days before Emmy's death, the Maxwells, in wheelchairs, went to the Chardin exhibition at the Metropolitan Museum. Two days before Emmy's death, and ten days before his own, Bill finished reading Tolstoy's novel. The events encompassed in that last month of their lives, the tenderness quietly exchanged among the friends who visited them were entirely consonant with the qualities of that departing pair: unforgettable, unforgotten.

Bill Maxwell said that he did not fear death but that he would miss reading novels. In his own novel *The Château,* the American protagonist passes his last day in Paris walking in autumnal light through streets and public gardens: "*I cannot leave!* he cried out silently to the old buildings and the brightness in the air, to the yellow leaves on the trees. *I cannot bear that all this will be here and I will not be.*"

Anthony Hecht

Time Will Darken It

WILLIAM MAXWELL's extraordinary novel *Time Will Darken It* takes its title from a text by Francisco Pacheco (1564–1654) about techniques employed in landscape painting, with particular reference to attaining perspective by rendering "three or four distances or planes." The Spanish painter (and teacher of Velázquez) describes the blocking or laying in of colors, declaring it best "to execute it directly in colour in order that the smalt may result brighter. If you temper the necessary quantity of pigment . . . with linseed or walnut oil and add enough white, you shall produce a bright tint. It must not be dark; on the contrary, it must be rather on the light side because time will darken it. . . ."

All of Maxwell's fiction is distinguished by a painterly eye of loyal fidelity to the smallest details, and his wife, Emily, to whom this novel is dedicated, was herself a painter. The Pacheco passage also hints at something deeply important about the novel's design: it begins with what seems a minor discord in domestic happiness and grows into something nearly hellish in its hallucinatory disorientation and emotional, as well as physical, anguish. It is a novel of domestic and social tyrannies of almost imperceptible subtlety, of motives so secret as to be unknown to those who harbor them, and, as distinct from other Maxwell novels, it employs an authorial voice of piercing wisdom, gentle irony, and thoughtful comment that sounds, time to time, like the voice of Chekhov.

There's a further reason that Chekhov comes to mind while reading *Time Will Darken It*. The book is divided into six parts, which in turn are subdivided into brief sections that run from as little as two to ten or twelve pages. Part 1, called "An Evening Party," runs to seven short sections and is the shortest part. Part 6, the final one, called "There Is a Remedy or There Is None," is the longest, with twenty-one sections, and there are ninety-two such sections in all. These sections, knit as they are into the complex narrative of the book, still retain qualities of independent coherence that make them seem like the suggestive, resonating, inconclusive short stories of Chekhov; an alert reader will everywhere be on the lookout for the subtlest inflections, the most delicate nuances; objects, rooms, toys, furniture are all allowed to speak, saying those things that humans darkly think but dare not utter or, sometimes, those things that humans don't even know they are thinking. Moreover, and again like Chekhov, it can be claimed that there are no minor characters in this novel. Admittedly, some have small parts to play, but the author is interested enough in all of them not to allow us to dismiss them as "minor." He recommends their histories, foibles, and thoughts to our notice, and takes pains with the least of them. There is in this a generous humanity that thickens the texture of this novel and enlarges its dimensions.

It has been said that Dickens is ill at ease and unconvincing when he attempts to portray tenderness between young couples; that Conrad seems at a loss in dealing with women; that Jane Austen has not much use for children in her fiction. No doubt any author has limitations, but in the works of William Maxwell there is an amplitude of sympathy that seems almost Russian. He presents few characters unworthy of sympathy; he does so with a good deal of authorial cunning. Quite early in this book we meet a woman named Mrs. Potter who seems intolerably self-centered, oblivious, assertive, and something of a bore. But the drama of the novel reveals her to be deeply vulnerable and touching in her distress. She is but one character among many from whom disguises are stripped away. The novel unfolds like a series of revelations, one within another, each semblance of reality proving a shell that opens upon a deeper, more painful truth.

William Maxwell inscribed a copy of his novel to us with these words: "This book is my cross-eyed child. It came out at the wrong time for it to be understood, and day after day there were letters from friends telling me how much they hated it. It was written too soon, perhaps, after analysis. In any case, I put the hero through more than he deserved, with an unkindness one reserves only for oneself."

It seems to me characteristic that Maxwell would be so hard on himself and/or on his hero, a lawyer named Austin King. King is the father of a four-year-old girl and the husband of a pregnant wife named Martha. He is, also, the son of a widely revered father, now dead, who was a judge of distinction and who, orphaned as a child, was brought up in Mississippi by a family named Potter, whose patriarch raised the boy on equal terms with his own five sons and toward whom Judge King felt a deep sense of love and obligation.

When the novel opens, Austin King has just received a letter addressed to his dead father in care of Austin's law firm. It is from a member of the Potter family who doesn't know the judge has died and who suggests that the broken threads of foster relations might be picked up and rewoven if Reuben Potter and his family visited Draperville, Illinois, where Judge King had settled and his son now lives. Austin has brooded and hesitated over this proposal, considering his wife's indisposition, as well as the obligation owed to his father (a formidable imago figure) and to the Potter foster family that raised and cared for the frightened, lonely boy who would in time become the distinguished judge. At the time of Austin's deliberations, we, the readers, scarcely know him. We assume that he has weighed all the pros and cons and, realizing that there is no perfect solution, has come to a decision that is at least plausible and disinterested. As perhaps he has. The decision he makes to invite the Potters, however, has absolutely catastrophic consequences for virtually everyone in the novel.

These are not consequences Austin King could possibly have foreseen. There is a Sophoclean destiny, mysterious and inevitable in its operation, that haunts even lesser, more peripheral characters. Take, for example, Rachel, the Kings' black cook and housekeeper. Her own home, where her children live with her, is invaded one day when she is away at work by a drunken black man "with no last name," who arrived by slow freight from Indianapolis. He has already frightened two fellow passengers in his boxcar simply by his appearance, and he strikes absolute terror in the hearts of Rachel's five children when he enters her shack and asks, "Where's your Ma?" He has been on the lam, wanted by police in St. Louis and Cincinnati, and he knows perfectly well where he is now, identifying himself to the children as their father:

> "Eugene, git up off of that couch and let your Pappy lie down. He's come a long way and he's tired. Your Ma fix me a little supper and then I'm going to sleep. I'm going to get in the bed and sleep for a week. Get up, you hear? Before I make you. You think you're grown, maybe, but you ain't grown enough. I show you. I show you right now."

What happened inside the shack was of no concern to the funeral basket, the two round stones, the coach lantern, and the coffeepot. They were merely the setting for a fancy-dress nightmare, not the actors. Evil moves about on two legs and has lines to speak, gestures that frighten because they are never completed. He can be blond, well bred, to all appearances gentle and kind. Or the eyes can be almond-shaped, the eyebrows plucked, the lids drooping. The hair can be kinky or curly or straight. Features and colouring are a matter of make-up to be left to the individual actor, who can, if he likes, with grease paint and eyebrow pencil create the face of a friend. If the actor wears a turban or a loincloth, the dramatic effect will be heightened, providing of course that the audience is not also wearing turbans and loincloths. What is important is that Evil be understood, otherwise the scene will not act. The audience will not be able to decide which character is evil and which is the innocent victim. It is quite simple, actually. The one comes to grief through no fault of his own, knows what is being done to him, and does not lift a hand to defend himself from the blow. If he defends himself, he is not innocent. The other has been offered a choice, and has chosen Evil. If the audience and the actors both remember this, they will have no trouble following or acting out the play, which should begin, in any case, quietly, in a low key, suggesting an atmosphere of peace and security and love. The funeral basket, the two round stones, the rain-rotted carriage seat, the coach lantern, and the coffeepot are very good. And for a backdrop let there be a quiet street on a November night in a small midwestern town. A woman comes down the street towards an arc light at the foot of a hill. Under her arm she has a brown paper parcel containing scraps of leftover food. A coloured woman, with her head down, her shoulders hunched, indicating that it is cold. If there is a wind-machine in the wings, the effect will be more realistic. There should be lights in the houses. The trees have shed their leaves. The woman stops suddenly and conveys to the audience by a look, by the absence of all expression, that a chill has passed over her which has nothing to do with the wind from the wings. She looks back at the arc light. And then she begins to run.

With enormous skill this passage suggests depths foreordained and darkened purposes. It is also cunning in its deliberately deceptive simplicities. When William Maxwell tells us, "It is quite simple, actually," we know, since we are more than halfway through the novel, that nothing is as simple as it first appears to be, and that Evil is by no means so easy to detect. It was not so for Oedipus. But look closely at the odds and ends of the setting, the pathetic miscellany of discarded objects that bear silent witness to the scene. Maxwell is attentive to these—the funeral basket, the coffeepot—as he is attentive throughout to the only slightly larger setting of his small Midwestern town. This is rendered at times with undisguised affection, and when we remember that William Maxwell was born in Lincoln, Illinois, in 1908, and that this novel is set in 1912, we understand that a cherished past is being delicately employed with incomparable fidelity as a ground for the terrible drama enacted in its midst. Maxwell's descriptive powers are richly present in all his fiction; his memory, his compassion, and his capacity to take note of even the smallest detail—all these are gifts that suggest his resemblance to certain of the Russians. But his Draperville, for all his love, is not free from blemish:

> Of the literary arts, the one most practised in Draperville was history. It was informal, and there was no reason to write it down since nothing was ever forgotten. The child born too soon after the wedding ceremony might learn to walk and to ride a bicycle; he might go to school and graduate into long pants, marry, move to Seattle, and do well for himself in the lumber business; but whenever his or his mother's name was mentioned, it was followed inexorably by some smiling reference to the date of his birth. No one knew what had become of the energetic secretary of the Chamber of Commerce who organized the Love-Thy-Neighbor-As-Thyself parade, but they knew why he left town shortly afterward, and history doesn't have to be complete. . . .
>
> The final work of shaping and selection was done by the Friendship Club. The eight regular members of this club were the high practitioners of history.

They met in rotation at one another's houses for luncheon and bridge. The food that they served was competitive and unwise, since many of them were struggling to maintain their figures. After the canned lobster or crabmeat, the tunafish baked in shells, the chicken patties, the lavish salads, the New York ice cream (all of which they would regret later), the club members settled down to bridge, with their hats on and their shoes pushed off under the card table, their voices rising higher and higher, their short-range view of human events becoming crueller and more malicious as they doubled and redoubled one another's bids, made grand slams, and quarrelled over the scoring. No reputation was safe with them, and only by being present every time could they hope to preserve their own. The innocent were thrown to the wolves, the kind made fun of, the old stripped of the dignity that belonged to their years. *They say* was the phrase invariably used when a good name was about to be auctioned off at the block. . . .

The flayed landscape of the western prairie does little to remind the people who live there of the covenant of works or the covenant of grace. The sky, visible right down to the horizon, has a diminishing effect upon everything in the foreground, and the distance is as featureless and remote as the possibility of punishment for slander. The roads run straight, with death and old age intersecting at right angles, and the harvest is stored in cemeteries.

If this does not sound like the landscape of a "cherished past," recall the Pacheco text and the phrase "time will darken it." Many more positive and beautiful descriptions of Draperville in all seasons of the year have already appeared before we reach the passage above. And we may recall that when the author said earlier that "it is quite simple, actually" to distinguish Evil from innocence, he was not being altogether straightforward. If this leads you to suppose that he is practicing deception upon his readers, or is careless of his art, you would be mistaken, having failed to grasp the point of view from which the novel is written.

Time Will Darken It is a novel of growing awareness on the part of many characters, but chiefly Austin King. Things begin "quietly, in a low key, suggesting an atmosphere of peace and security and love." To be sure, there is domestic friction at the start; Austin and Martha are not speaking—or, rather, she is not speaking to him. But that rift seems to be quickly resolved, so that by the end of the third section, "they held each other and lost themselves in the opening, unmasking tenderness that always comes after a satisfactory quarrel." The rest of the novel will prove such breezy confidence unfounded. The delusion is that of a man who, early in this tale, has little or no knowledge of himself. Illumination grows as the novel progresses, not only for Austin but for many others. He will go on to find himself—he who prides himself on being a model of rectitude—virtually incriminated by a land deal proposed to his friends and neighbors by his guest, the visiting Reuben Potter, whose visit, with wife and two children, lasts over a month, and who, failing to persuade Austin to invest in the deal (which turns out to be dishonest), nevertheless gets him to draw up the legal papers (without charge) in which his gullible neighbors signify their participation. Austin's understanding grows all too slowly, and some of what appear to be false leads early in the novel, optimistic expectations, even lyric descriptions of Midwestern small-town life in a winter that conceals all flaws under a mantle of the purest snow, turn out to be views of a man who does not really know himself, and consequently does not really know others. As we move along we gradually come to see, as he learns himself to see, Austin's almost blind fatuity that had hampered him in all his relations, not least those that bound him to his wife, and his failure to take seriously enough the peculiar behavior of the Potter daughter, Nora. But the point of view is not simply Austin's, though he is the most responsible character in the story. There is also the child's point of view. Austin's daughter, Abbey, is four years old. The age is itself significant. The novel is set in 1912, when Maxwell was four years old, and much of the lyric tenderness we encounter in these pages may be ascribed to this small biographical coincidence. Abbey has a point of view of her own, as all children do; and early in this story she is exposed to a shameless account by Mrs. Potter of her own marital infidelity, an account that the ears of a child should certainly have been spared.

During this recital, Ab sat as still as a stone. In those moments when life is a play and not merely a backstage rehearsal, children are the true audience. With no lines to speak, they remain politely on their side of the proscenium unless (after the hero has blinded himself with his own hands) the playwright chooses to have one or two of them led onto the stage to be wept over and then frightened with some such blessing as *May heaven be kinder to you than it has been to me*. Although children are not always equipped to understand all that they see and overhear, they know as a rule which character is supposed to represent Good and which Evil, and they appreciate genuine repentance. By all rights, when the play is finished, the actors should turn and bow to them, and ask for their applause.

Any reader who can read these words without a sense of compassionate irony will have missed the tenor and tone of William Maxwell's brilliant novel.

Angel Child

"I WISH I HAD had a larger talent," William Maxwell said, regretting that he had been "so repetitious in my work." This is typically Maxwellian—shrewdly preemptive, leaving it to his reader to protest: Isn't it only the large talent that can return to the same source, the same "material" (his term), the same characters and central events, and make of them, each time, a new and complex work of art? Isn't his the obsessive, self-defining recurrence we expect in our major poets, a project both human and grand?

W. H. Auden's criterion for "major poet" was that one could date the work. And certainly Maxwell's growth as a writer, the deepening complexity of what he wrote, can be tracked through the structure used and the choice of a writing style. It is not a purely technical choice, although technique is essential: it suggests a set of moral as well as aesthetic values, which is, in skillful hands, hard to detect without analyzing the components of the style, looking at the work sentence by sentence, which was, in Maxwell, increasingly how it was made.

But first I need to tell you what had happened. His most succinct account of it is the middle one, chronologically (*Ancestors,* 1971), the one that most overtly claimed nonfictional, factual ground:

> My mother spent certain days of the week rolling gauze bandages, in a white uniform, her black hair covered by a white scarf with a red cross on it. My father drilled with a group of local businessmen. . . .
>
> . . . My mother drove the car in the night parade on Armistice Day and my father sat astride the bonnet, smiling and waving to everybody. . . .
>
> I was aware that I had lived through an important moment of history. I know now but I didn't know then that the less people have to do with history the better. Our whole family came down with Spanish influenza during the epidemic of 1918—my mother and father in a hospital in Bloomington, where my mother had gone to have my younger brother, and where she died three days after he was born.

"Spanish influenza" was the most ruthlessly efficient devastation the world has yet seen, killing over thirty million people in a single year, healthy adults along with the old and the weak—"It was relentless," Maxwell said. Despite its popular name, it did not originate in Spain (only the earliest reports of it did) but, most likely, in U.S. Army training camps. When the recruits were shipped to the front, so was the contagion, which adapted to its new environments and reinfected the carriers, who brought it home. In the last four months of 1918, U.S. civilian deaths from influenza and pneumonia, its frequent complication, registered up to eighteen times the estimated normal number. In Chicago, transportation hub for the upper Midwest where the Maxwells lived, 1,566 deaths were expected; actual deaths—10,755, with one group disproportionately represented: pregnant women.

Blossom Blinn and William Keepers Maxwell were married in June 1903. They lived in Lincoln, Illinois, across the street from one set of in-laws and around the corner from the other. William Maxwell was their second child, born in August 1908. He weighed four pounds at birth, even less at six weeks; allergic to his mother's milk, he was so frail he was carried around on a pillow. At the time of her third pregnancy, Blossom was thirty-eight, and with reports of widespread sickness now everywhere, the decision was made for William's parents to take the train to a better hospital, about thirty miles away, for her last weeks of lying-in. Annette, Blossom's sister and a family favorite, was to stay with the children; when she was suddenly called to Chicago, they were hustled off to Aunt Maybel—decidedly not a favorite—who lived with Grandmother Maxwell. That house was dark and dour, "not a place either of us would have chosen to be sick in," and on Christmas Day "my brother and I both came down with the disease that was raging everywhere around us."

The first account Maxwell made of this intersection with history was fully dramatized in *They Came Like Swallows* (1937), his second novel. He said each novel evolved from a central metaphor, and that for *Swallows* he pictured a stone thrown into a pond, creating a widening circle of ripples, and then a second stone thrown inside that circle to create another, and then another—an apt figure as well for the war and the successive waves of the pandemic. The novel is divided into three sections, or Books, each with its own close-third-person point of view: Bunny; Robert, his older brother; and their father, James. The first section centers on Armistice Day, November 11, 1918; the third unfolds over twenty-four hours in the early New Year 1919 (when, Maxwell wrote, his childhood ended); and the middle, the longest, covers the weeks in between. These restrictions of time and place (two houses, only blocks apart), and the high incidence of scene within them, reinforce drama—Acts I, II, and III.

That first section was revised eight times, according to Maxwell, before he could go forward with Books II and III, and again, apparently, before the reissue of *Swallows* in 1988. (I quote from that later edition.) The section "Whose Angel Child" opens in innocence, as the first stone disturbs the placid surface of the pond. Although Elizabeth Morison is seven months pregnant,

Bunny hasn't noticed; he learns about the baby by watching his mother sew:

> "If they aren't tea towels, what are they?"
> He waited impatiently while she bit off the thread and measured a new length from her spool.
> "Diapers."
> The word started a faint spinning of excitement within him. He went thoughtfully and sat down beside his mother in the window seat. From there he could see the side yard and the fence, the Koenigs' yard, and the side of the Koenigs' white house. The Koenigs were German but they couldn't help that, and they had a little girl whose name was Anna. In January Anna would be a year old. Mr. Koenig got up very early to help with the washing before he went to work. The washing-machine galumpty-lumped, galumpty-lumped, at five o'clock in the morning. By breakfast time there would be a string of white flags blowing in the autumn wind. They weren't flags, of course; they were diapers. And that was just it. People never made diapers unless somebody was going to have a baby.

In these short, direct sentences, each action or observation is given equal importance, whether the sound of the machine or a baby coming. In that full paragraph, there are fourteen discrete independent clauses, each complete, self-contained, with its own subject and predicate. These sentences are also arranged unfailingly in "normal order," the subject and predicate put first, except for three brief phrases ("From there . . . ," "In January . . . ," "By breakfast time . . ."). Even when the sentence opens up into more detail (and there are two subordinate clauses used as adverbs at sentence end), the position of greatest attention—the head of the sentence—has been reserved for actions and assertions. As an enacted scene, this one is slight, and full of narrative summary, but feels extended because the syntax is committed to clarity, rather than complication, and to drama.

Meanwhile, point of view, setting, and plot are faithful to autobiographical as well as historical data. The house—the layout of the rooms, the furnishings, the lot it sits on, and the neighborhood—is the very house on Ninth Street in Lincoln described so fully in *Ancestors*; and the people will recur, easily recognized, in most of his books. At age twenty-five, he wrote in the preface to the *Collected Stories*:

three-quarters of the material I would need for the rest of my writing life was already at my disposal. My father and mother. My brothers. The cast of larger-than-life-size characters—affectionate aunts, friends of the family, neighbors white and black—that I was presented with when I came into the world. The look of things. The weather. Men and women long at rest in the cemetery but vividly remembered. The Natural History of home: the suede glove on the front-hall table, the unfinished game of solitaire, the oriole's nest suspended from the tip of the outermost branch of the elm tree, dandelions in the grass. All there, waiting for me to learn my trade and recognize instinctively what would make a story or sustain the complicated cross-weaving of longer fiction.

Maxwell made central this world, and the events that overwhelmed it, in three books written over four decades, and his distinct treatments supply a rare case study in the transformation of received material into art. We should not, however, assign them a false hierarchy. To begin with, the usual genre expectations do not apply. *Ancestors* often reads more like biography than memoir, while in *So Long, See You Tomorrow* (1980) the narrator refers to "This memoir—if that's the right name for it. . . ." There is also, in that "novel," this assertion:

> What we, or at any rate what I, refer to confidently as memory—meaning a moment, a scene, a fact that has been subjected to a fixative and thereby rescued from oblivion—is really a form of storytelling that goes on continually in the mind and often changes with the telling. Too many conflicting emotional interests are involved for life ever to be wholly acceptable, and possibly it is the work of the storyteller to rearrange things so that they conform to this end. In any case, in talking about the past we lie with every breath we draw.

• • •

IT STANDS AS a caution: comparison of the separate accounts should remain an examination of "rearrangements," three forms of storytelling. Where he departs from or reimagines autobiography is simply a useful place to begin.

Most of the departures, insofar as we can track them, occur in *Swallows,* and they seem to be, like its structure, in the service of drama. Bunny is not ten, as Maxwell was in 1918, but eight, an adjustment made perhaps to emphasize his delicacy. Bunny is devoutly, obsessively dependent on his mother while wary of his father, who often reads aloud to his wife newspaper reports about the war and the influenza. At the same time, danger is brought close to home by Arthur Cook, a sick boy in Bunny's classroom. The second departure is even more significant. Bunny's section ends on November 12; his father is reading aloud:

> [b]ut instead of listening to the military terms of the armistice with Germany, Bunny went and put his head in his mother's lap, for he felt very odd inside of him. He heard her say, "James, this child is burning up with fever!" and he thought dreamily that it must be so.

By dividing the children's illnesses one from the other in his story line, what Maxwell gains is an opportunity not only for scene but for narrative, appeasing its need for events over time, their sequence, and their consequence.

In Book II, as national contagion broadens, domestic danger is narrowed, and not just for fragile Bunny:

> Standing in the door to the library, his father said, "It is vitally important to keep her out of that boy's room. 'Tie her down,' Dr. Macgregor said, 'if you can't keep her out any other way.'"

Thus ground is prepared for the coruscating blame, regret, and guilt that are common to survivors of tragedy and characteristic of Maxwell's fiction.

By the end of 1918, information disseminated about the flu paired sound public-health advice (the quarantine of victims) with absurdly desperate remedies and precautions. Legislation in San Francisco required surgical masks to be worn on the trolley—but allowed their removal in crowded shops and restaurants. Newspapers as well as gossip promulgated useless salves and nostrums along with the widespread belief that Germans had brought the germ to the States in submarines. With no scientific understanding of cause, much less remedy, suspicion mixed freely with superstition, and helplessness both pervasive and real made a casual remark seem, in hindsight, prophetic. *They Came Like Swallows, Time Will Darken It, Ancestors,* and *So Long, See You Tomorrow* all contain the mother's three presentiments of her death. What appears only in *Swallows* is an event made possible by separating the illnesses:

"There's a bird in here," Irene exclaimed and went back into the sick-room again, closing the door behind her.

His mother turned to him, her arms filled with winter underwear. "You'll have to do something, Robert."

This was more like it. . . . Robert slid down the stepladder, recklessly, having made up his mind to try the broom first. Then if that didn't work, they'd have to let him use his bee-bee gun.

When he came back upstairs, Irene and his mother were both in Bunny's room—Irene by the dresser and his mother on the edge of Bunny's bed, holding him. With feverish sick eyes, Bunny was watching the sparrow that flew round and round the room in great wide frightened swings.

In folklore, a bird in the house forecasts a death. This one lets Maxwell not merely report on superstition but dramatize it: Robert will blame himself when his mother falls ill, although it is Robert, not his mother, who catches the flu from Bunny.

Meanwhile, a more rational warning is introduced in Book II as well:

"[T]he schools will be closed until further notice . . ." Robert felt very small prickles in the region of his spine. He read the first sentence twice, to make sure that there had not been a mistake. . . . [The notice] meant that something was happening in town, all

around him. Not an open excitement like the day
the Armistice was signed, with fire engines and whis-
tles and noise and people riding around in the
hearse. But a quiet thing that he couldn't see or
hear; that was in Bunny's room, and on Tenth Street
where Arthur Cook lived, and more places than that.
. . . The Illinois committee on public safety strongly . . . cau-
tions people against gathering in large numbers for any
purpose, also traveling on railroad trains except when
absolutely necessary. . . .

Superstition is the mind's defense against chaos; so is
blame. And both are fueled by powerlessness. What the
child understands utterly the adults disregard, and that
blindness, or willfulness, or carelessness, will apparently
obsess the adult William Maxwell throughout his life, as
it does the surrogate for his father in *Swallows:*

> If he could only go back, if he could remember
> everything during the last ten days, why then he
> might—it was foolish of course, but the same idea
> occurred to him over and over—he might be able to
> change what had already happened.

Throughout the middle section, impending tragedy
is paced for maximum suspense: Dr. Macgregor tells
Elizabeth that Bunny, her "angel child," is going to get
well; Robert hears the train whistle and knows "all in
one miserable second that his father and mother were
on that train; that they had gone away and left him . . . ;

and that he would not see them again for a long time, if ever." Later:

> [Robert] was cut loose. He was adrift utterly in his own sickness.
>
> For three days and three nights it was like that.
>
> Aunt Clara appeared every two hours—now fully dressed, and now in a long white nightgown with her hair in braids down her back. Sometimes her coming was so slight an interruption that he could not be sure afterwards whether she had been there at all. Again she stood beside his bed for an indefinite time, with two white tablets in one hand and a glass of water in the other.

As in Act II of any good play, new danger overlaps the current one, when Robert learns his parents "both have the flu, and they're very sick," his mother with double pneumonia. Robert's fever breaks, but the end of Book II fulfills all its presentiments nevertheless:

> He followed [Aunt Clara] into Grandmother Morison's room. Bunny was there alone. And he was in his pajamas. Aunt Clara sat down in the rocking-chair and gathered Bunny onto her lap.
>
> "It's about your mother," she said.
>
> Her voice sounded hoarse, as if she had a cold. She began to rock back and forth, back and forth, until her eyes covered over with tears. Robert turned then and went out of the room.

He did not have to be told what had happened. He knew already. During the night while he was sleeping, she got worse. Then she did not have an even chance, like the doctor said. And she died. His mother was dead.

A fairly good measure of dramatic effectiveness—the vividness of a scene—is its plausible pacing: events seem to happen in real time, as though we watch them happen. Here, Maxwell accomplishes this by alternating simple actions, dialogue, and description, most of it rendered in the short, direct sentences, subject and verb placed first, that dominate the prose. But the final paragraph is completely in Robert's head, paced solely by a different kind of sentence. First there is a pair of clauses roughly equal in length, but unequal in grammatical importance—one provides subject and predicate, the fundament, the engine of the sentence ("He did not have to be told"); and one, grammatically subordinate ("what had happened"), functions as a noun, the object of that predicate. Sentence 2 is the simplest possible assertion—subject, verb, and modifier: "He knew already." The next two sentences supply a brief delay—a pause framed by subordinate clauses ("During the night while he was sleeping . . . like the doctor said"). Then comes the relentless repetition, again in short, direct sentences, closing the lid of the box: "And she died. His mother was dead." This paragraph has no necessary narrative information to convey—Clara's tears have told us what they "told" Robert—but Maxwell chooses the virtues of exposition, its authority, its directness. There is no action, no description, no dialogue, only the unappeasable clarity of such news in the mind of a child.

Syntax—the order of the words in a sentence—is a rhythmic system. It is also a structure, shaping the information it contains and disseminates. Narrative plot line and dramatic scene are other, larger structures. Narrative introduces and develops action and detail which often cause, or whose significance is revealed by, later action and detail; their occurrence over time is crucial, and is the source of momentum *(what happened next?)*. Dramatic structure enacts; it restricts information to a sustained "present moment" of unknown outcome, making action and detail immediate. *Swallows* is a powerful example of conventional novel structure: events occurring over time and organized—released to us—in dramatic scenes. In addition, Maxwell uses a dramatic syntax, placing the subject and predicate first in his short equivalent sentences: the predicates—the actions—dominate, and we are made witnesses to the events, as in a play.

When Maxwell wrote again about the epidemic, over thirty years later, he did so with a very different kind of sentence, and a different large structure. In *Ancestors,* his mother's death is not the dramatic climax, as in *Swallows,* but announced, like a thesis statement in an essay. The overall structure of the account is exposition, and the focus is not on event but on knowledge:

> In her cotton nightgown, with her hair in a braid down her back, [Aunt Maybel] appeared beside my

bed every three hours during the night. Without speaking but with, nevertheless, a look of concern on her face for which I was grateful, she held out a glass of water and the pills the family doctor had left for me. A rock doesn't have to be congenial if it is the only one there is to cling to. Sometimes it was my uncle who came, instead. And they were also, of course, taking care of my brother, who was in the big brass bed in the spare room. Time passed by in jerks. I woke to a grey winter light, in that little room with my uncle's desk and typewriter and all the grim-faced ancestors looking down on the progress of my fever, and remembered things I had overheard my aunt saying on the telephone downstairs in the dining room, and was frightened, and closed my eyelids for a second to shut out thoughts I couldn't deal with, and when I opened them again it was black outside the windows. If only people would say to children when something unbearable happens, *Now you are growing up . . . This is how it comes about,* it might help, I think. It might have the same alleviating effect that being able to recognize the fact that you are dreaming does, when you are in the grip of a nightmare.

One morning the telephone rang quite early, before my aunt brought my breakfast to me, and I heard enough to know that she was talking to my father in Bloomington, and that there was something he wanted her to do for him. A little later she called my brother and me into my grandmother's room. It was the first time I had seen him since we were taken sick, and we hardly looked at each other. We were in alien country. My aunt sat down in a low rocking chair and took me on her lap, and I knew when her eyes filled with tears what she was going to say, but it had to be put into words and she did that too. What had to be done she could be counted on to do.

Here, the short declaratives, dominant in *Swallows,* are as rare as raisins in a poor man's pudding:

> Sometimes it was my uncle who came, instead.
> Time passed by in jerks.
> We were in alien country.

The sentence with Maybel's hair, a detail also in *Swallows,* is one of the two others that contain just a single clause. There is also this: "A little later she called my brother and me into my grandmother's room." These five sentences form the spine of the crucial event, a narrative précis. Elsewhere, with narrative information to be conveyed—"what had happened"—the listing is so rapid the prose feels quite breathless:

> I woke to a grey winter light, in that little room with my uncle's desk and typewriter and all the grim-faced ancestors . . . and remembered things . . . and was frightened, and closed my eyelids for a second. . . .

But all of these sentences just quoted are exceptions to the primary pattern; instead of the repeating parity in *Swallows,* Maxwell's sentences in *Ancestors* enact a hierarchy. The primary action ("she held out a glass of water and the pills") is connected within the sentence to other clauses, with their own subjects and predicates ("for which I was grateful," "the pills the family doctor had left for me")—clauses that do not express a complete thought and are dependent on, subordinate to, the one that does. Throughout the passage, most of the information released is restricted, hedged, contextualized, qualified, disputed, or worried over with a subordinate clause placed either before the subject and predicate or after them or both ("Without speaking but with, nevertheless, a look of concern on her face for which I was grateful, she held out a glass of water and the pills the family doctor had left for me"). And there is another syntactic fingerprint: sometimes, one of those weaker clauses is used as a noun, and may even be set in the foreground ("*What had to be done* she could be counted on to do").

Hierarchical sentences, made with grammatically unequal clauses, are called "hypotactic," and hypotaxis is how adults think, how we make meaning: except in the wake of trauma, pieces of information are not left confusingly equal but sorted by the brain into value-laden relation to one another. In the passage above, Maxwell uses the main clause to foreground and empower not the events, as in *Swallows* ("Mr. Koenig got up very early. . . . ," "The washing-machine galumpty-lumped. . . ."), but a mind trying to reconstruct those events ("I didn't know then," "I think probably what happened"). First allegiance is to complexity, no matter the dramatic cost.

The guideline for effective dramatic prose may be: Why two words when one will deliver a greater punch? The goal is to honor immediacy. The guideline here might be: Why one oversimplifying noun or modifier when a subordinate clause, with its additional verb, will be more precise or inclusive? The goal is to honor moral complication. The latter helps explain the extraordinary authenticity and authority of Maxwell's last novel, where a third account of the tragedy appears, again "rearranged" into exposition and with almost no scenic element at all, no attempt to dramatize "what had happened." It is as though he had put aside the first project, whereby we might witness the loss and also grieve, and showed us in *Ancestors* the one who grieves, and then, finally, in *So Long, See You Tomorrow*, the one who, unaccountably, survives that grief. And the writing style, while still recognizably his, changes yet again.

So Long, See You Tomorrow was written, Maxwell said, literally sentence by sentence, every sentence auditioned in the unfolding text until the exact location for it had been found. Particularly in the first half of the book, most of these sentences use the strategies perfected in *Ancestors,* elaborated even further for his first-person retrospective narrator. His preference is still "normal" order—fundament first—but now the sentences extend themselves through a string of subordinate clauses: this accommodates not only an increased amount of information but also an exactitude of detail and proportion. Chapter 2 begins:

> I very much doubt that I would have remembered for more than fifty years the murder of a tenant farmer I never laid eyes on if (1) the murderer hadn't been the father of somebody I knew, and (2) I hadn't later on done something I was ashamed of afterward.

There are seven clauses in that opening sentence. And here are the fourth and fifth sentences, with four and six clauses, respectively:

> When my father was getting along in years and the past began to figure more in his conversation, I asked him one day what my mother was like. I knew what she was like as my mother but I thought it was time somebody told me what she was like as a person.

And the next sentence—the longest in the second paragraph—contains this little gem of sequential subordination, like those Russian dolls nestled one within the other:

> whether he didn't after all this time have any feeling about her much, or did have but didn't think he ought to.

This syntax simply refuses to presume.

The same patterns are at work in the fourth paragraph also, where Maxwell uses subordinate clauses in every possible position in the sentence—before the fundament, after it, interrupting it, and as adverbs ("when . . . ," "where . . ."), as grammatical object, and even as the subject of the sentence:

> I was so small when these things happened that either I did not know about them or else I didn't feel them because they took place at one remove, so to speak. When my brother undressed at night he left his artificial leg leaning against a chair. It was as familiar to me, since we slept in the same room, as his cap or his baseball glove. He was not given to feeling sorry for himself, and older people were always careful not to show their sorrow over what had happened to him. What I felt about his "affliction" was tucked away in my unconscious mind (assuming there is such a thing) where I couldn't get at it.

In the above, there are sixteen clauses—but unlike in *Swallows,* ten are subordinate. Meanwhile, the qualifiers we saw in *Ancestors* proliferate: "either . . . or else," "so to speak," "assuming there is such a thing." The narrator is made trustworthy by virtue of his discrimination, inclusiveness, and right proportion.

Paragraph 4 has another function as well: like the pause that delays the news of the mother's death in

Swallows, here hypotaxis interrupts and delays a catalogue, family disasters that occurred "between 1909 and 1919":

> My grandfather, spending the night in a farmhouse, was bitten on the ear by a rat or a ferret and died three months later of blood poisoning. My mother's only brother was in an automobile accident and lost his right arm. My mother's younger sister poured kerosene on a grate fire that wouldn't burn and set fire to her clothing and bore the scars of this all the rest of her life. My older brother, when he was five years old, got his foot caught in a turning carriage wheel. [Paragraph 3]

> My younger brother was born on New Year's Day, at the height of the influenza epidemic of 1918. My mother died two days later of double pneumonia. [Opening of paragraph 5]

In a later chapter, the narrator will say, "I would be content to stick to the facts if there were any." Paragraphs 3 and 5 contain the "facts" of the back story, the first circle of ripples into which the second stone—the murder of Lloyd Wilson—is thrown. And these facts are rendered in the same short, direct sentences Maxwell used earlier, simple declaratives and compounds, each player given his or her own independent clause ("My grandfather," "my mother's only brother," "my mother's younger sister," "my older brother," "my younger brother," "my mother"). But this time that syntax is not the pattern but a variation, a brief exception. What follows the catalogue is a compound containing an important subordinate clause: "The worst *that could happen* had happened, and the shine went out of everything." And the next sentence, having begun with another sort of catalogue— those breathless compounds again—ends in subordination, to form a transition:

> Disbelieving, we endured the wreath on the door, and the undertaker coming and going, the influx of food, the overpowering odor of white flowers, and all the rest of it, including the first of a series of housekeepers, *who took care of the baby and sat in my mother's place at mealtime.*

Now the prose resumes its careful dance of clauses, of speculation and assertion:

> Looking back I think it more than likely that long before she ever laid eyes on us that sallow-faced, flat-chested woman had got the short end of the stick. She came from a world we knew nothing about, and I don't remember that she ever had any days off. She may have made a stab at being a mother to my older brother and me, but it would have taken a good deal more than that to break through our resistance.

With the narrator's credentials established within the prose style, we accord tremendous authority to the final assertion (again with a crucial subordinate clause) and its one, unconsoled adjective: "We knew *what we had had*, and were not going to be taken in by any form of counterfeit affection."

Paragraph 5 predicts the overall structure of the novel. Again and again, Maxwell will use syntax to counter omniscience:

> I very much doubt that . . .
> I had to guess . . .
> I would have thought . . .
> I have no way of knowing . . .
> I suspect that . . .
> I doubt if . . .
> [I]t would have been strange if . . .
> I could not tell whether . . .

With such fundaments, what was thought, believed, suspected, or "known" is rendered subordinate, tentative, open to challenge. This syntactic choice, which in effect enacts the narrator's many overt warnings (that there are no facts, that "in talking about the past we lie"), dominates the entire first half of the book. And even after the meticulous narrator exits the novel, taking his first-person pronoun with him, not to return until the last six pages, letting the reconstructed murder of Lloyd Wilson unfold uninterrupted in scene after dramatic scene—even then, that stylistic, indeed moral, compunction lingers in a kind of syntactic footprint, those clausal parts of speech:

He knew *what had been done to him* but not *what he had done to deserve it.*

Whether they are part of home or home is part of them is not a question children are prepared to answer.

Whether she would have accepted Clarence if she hadn't been sick with love for a man she couldn't have was a question she had never until now tried to answer.

And the novel leaves us in the same conditional wonderment where it began, with a sentence fragment composed entirely of multiple subordinate clauses:

And whether the series of events that started with the murder of Lloyd Wilson—whether all that finally began to seem less real, more like something he dreamed, so that instead of being stuck there he could go on and by the grace of God lead his own life, undestroyed by what was not his doing.

Poet George Oppen in *Of Being Numerous* makes a claim for "Clarity / In the sense of transparence, / I don't mean that much can be explained." Very little about the influenza pandemic could be explained, but through Maxwell's three distinct transparent writing styles, we can see the loss, the grief, and then the scar. The power and authenticity of these accounts do not derive merely from what is called "poetry of witness."

Apparently compelled back into memory ("if he could remember everything . . . he might be able to change what had already happened"), and then forward into understanding (so that he could "lead his own life, undestroyed"), he was also scrupulous about their limitations, making these as clear in his work as what memory and insight had uncovered.

The source of that moral stringency is harder to detect but may be surmised from two specific, anomalous occasions, written perhaps before resolve grew firm. The first is *Ancestors*'s Chapter 17, inserted between his mother's death and the grieving months that followed, a shimmering third-person visitation by "a man and a woman—both young, in their early thirties—and a little boy." This is an affectionate, lyrical, dreamy divagation, a long prose poem, an album of images—fishing on the river, riding in the sleigh or horse-drawn cart, the white lilac bush, a corduroy suit, the aging family dog—a childhood released from narrative and the cruel progression of time.

The second, however, another rescue, uses narrative—and fiction's sleight of hand. In another early novel set in the house on Ninth Street, *Time Will Darken It* (he called the book "my cross-eyed child" in the flyleaf of my copy), there is life-threatening childbirth but no influenza (the year is 1912), and the mother survives. "It's just a matter of love," he said in a late interview, "of emotional attachment. For some people, love matters more than anything. With lots of people, it doesn't at all. For me it did. And does." Pressed by a therapist—" 'if your mother were alive, if you could talk to her, what would you say?' "—"what I said was, 'Here are these beautiful books, that I made for you.' "

Richard Bausch

Grace

I FIRST MET Bill Maxwell as a result of a cancellation. That is, someone—I no longer recall who—backed out of a performance at the prestigious reading series of the Library of Congress, and an acquaintance of mine who had worked at the library for years called me to ask if I'd be willing to read with William Maxwell. I was thrilled, of course, and only slightly troubled that this was happening because someone else couldn't be there. I had read Mr. Maxwell's stories, the ones collected in the volume *Over By the River*. The photo of him on the back shows him concentrating, looking over something either he or someone else has written. He looks stern in the photo, and rather big. I'd envisioned a tall man, imposing and, for me, scary. I don't know why this is so.

Meeting writers whose work I have loved is ever a faintly anxiety-laden thing for me—perhaps because I have always felt that someone with that sort of vision would immediately see through my doubts to the frightened creature under my heart, the one that suspects my work to be clumsy and obvious, and my talent to be fraudulent. That creature.

I remember I wrote my pal Charles Baxter to tell him I was going to read with Maxwell and was both frightened and excited about the prospect. He wrote a lovely thing back, saying he envied me for the honor and saying some wonderful things about William Maxwell's work, one line of which I recall exactly: "To begin with, he has never written a bad sentence." I liked that, and I thought Mr. Maxwell would like it. So I took it with me, and at the library, where I was introduced as the author of *The* Fisher*man's Wife* (the book is called *The* Fire*man's Wife*), I stood up and began my reading by saying that I wanted the whole evening to be in honor of Mr. Maxwell, who was seated in the front row and was gazing at me with his kindly eyes. I don't believe I have ever seen a man more delicate-looking, and I do not mean simply his age; there was something so completely fine about his features and his manner, I felt as if I had come into the ken of a separate order of being than my own, and while I am quite aware of the idolatrous sound of that, I can't find a better way of expressing how it felt to see him and shake hands with him that first time. Say that I was out of the street, and he was royalty, except that *he* never behaved that way. That was just how it felt, being aware of his work, of what he knew and had seen of the world, and finding myself the receiver of his immense graciousness.

At any rate, I read Charlie's words about him to the audience and then went on and read a story of my own (it was "Consolation," which, not long before this, had been in *The New Yorker*—Bill's magazine, as we all know).

When he stepped to the podium to read, he said a few kindly things about the life, as he put it, that he saw in my story and about the pleasing coincidence that my characters were from Illinois. Then he read some of the wonderful tales from *The Old Man at the Railroad Crossing*, his voice clear and resonant and strong, though very soft, too. After this, everyone adjourned to a big room to mingle. There was wine and cheese and fruit. A lot of friends had come to see me read, but of course—and quite rightly—almost everyone was there to see William Maxwell, and so I spoke only briefly with him. He asked if he could have a copy of Charlie's letter. I gave him that and the copy of *The Fireman's Wife* that I had read from. We exchanged a few pleasantries about Illinois, the fact that he had grown up there and taught briefly at the University of Illinois, where I had met my wife, Karen, twenty-three years earlier.

That summer, I was at the National Academy of Arts and Letters to receive an award, and I saw him again. I remember being stunned once more by the delicate look of him—he stood about to my shoulder. We shook hands, and he asked how I was, how things were going, and he did so in that tone he could use that made you know he wasn't speaking rhetorically, and so I found myself telling him—confiding in him, really—that in fact I was just then quite chagrined at having discovered a malapropism in my just-published novel, *Rebel Powers.* He leaned into me, smiling, as if telling me a secret, and said in his soft voice, "You know, Richard, perfection is an illusion." Then he seemed to consider this, nodding a little. "Besides, they'll probably be puzzling out what you must have meant, anyway." (For months after this pass, I found myself being more tolerant in traffic—his voice would come to me saying the words "perfection is an illusion.")

Perhaps a year later, I wrote him a letter to tell him how much I admired his book *Ancestors: A Family History.* I thought that since he probably had to contend with letters from dozens of people who assume he recalls everyone he meets, and because I myself am plagued with a terrible memory for names, I should remind him where we met and what the circumstances were. He fired back a letter gently scolding me for supposing he wouldn't remember me. "I'm not so old as all that," he said. I wrote back to say I was actually supposing he might be like me, and our correspondence began. During that same period, he and Charlie Baxter also struck up a correspondence—a fact of which I am very proud. His letters to me were always brief, but filled with details and lovely phrases about what he liked, what he was at present appreciating about the life around him, and the reading he was doing (nobody read more than Bill, or got more out of it). Karen and I were headed to Italy, and he wrote me about the drawings of Michelangelo in the basement of the sacristy behind San Lorenzo in Florence. "It is almost like being close enough to him to reach out and touch him," he wrote. And we went there, and it was just as Bill said it was.

And when Emmy, his wife, broke her leg, he wrote me to say, "I'm sure a time will come when we'll look back on this and smile."

He was eighty-seven, writing that.

That year, 1995, the actor and director Bob Balaban was going to have a celebratory and inaugural screening of the movie he'd adapted from my novel *The Last Good Time*. I called Bill and asked if he and Emmy would like to come along. We would meet in a little Italian restaurant—Patsy's, Frank Sinatra's old hangout on Fifty-sixth and Broadway, three or four blocks from the theater. Bill said he'd have to check with Emmy, and so I gave him the address, and we left it at that.

My eldest daughter, Emily, and I drove to New York that chilly early April weekend, and we convened at Patsy's with several friends, including my publisher and a couple of editors I knew. We had a bottle of Merlot, and I assumed that Bill hadn't been able to make it. But then one of the folks at the table said to me, "Isn't that William Maxwell?"

I turned, and there he was, with Emmy, standing just inside the door, scanning that crowded room. They were dressed for winter, and he wore a rough-looking old gray fedora, which he removed as I stood and waved and hurried over there. Immediately Emmy began to apologize for the unreliability of answer machines and the difficulty of getting a cab at rush hour in New York. I don't think I have ever seen a more beautiful woman, and she was then seventy-five years old. They made such an impressive couple, standing there in the confusion, so solicitous of each other and of me.

There was some trouble about the table. The waiter had seated us at a smaller one, and it was going to take some adjustment to get us all together. Bill quickly offered to get a separate table, and I'm afraid I turned to the waiter and said, low, "We're going to get these two in with us, bub, or I'm gonna make a scene in here you don't want to witness."

I don't think Bill ever knew this, and of course he would've been horrified by it.

At any rate, we did all sit together and we had a fine dinner, and he drank a cold beer, saying it was the first one in years and it tasted very good. We talked a little about the depredations of the academy, and I described for him some of the idiocies that were becoming rife in the universities then. All the myriad "isms" on which people were spending their intellectual coinage. He kept using the phrase that I believe best expresses where the peculiar graciousness of his kind comes from: "Shame on them," he'd say. And he meant it (and where, in our present soup of victim mentality, do we find that word used with any true feeling in it at all anymore?).

While we were walking down Broadway to the site of the screening, I mentioned that I had just finished reading *They Came Like Swallows,* and that the book—which draws heavily on the death of his mother in 1918, when he was ten years old—took me apart and then put me back together again. He glanced at me and his eyes had welled, and then he resumed walking, head down. "It was written in tears," he said. I thought about how a man could still hurt over something that had happened seventy-five years earlier, and my heart raced. There was something almost exhilarating about it—it was what I've come to think of as a species-thrill. *This is what it really is, being human.*

I wish I could explain this better. I simply can't.

We walked on and spoke about our ancestors (I had little idea where mine came from, Ireland mostly—the joke I make accounting for my name is that one German got over the wall on the paternal side a couple of generations back; on both sides of my family there are Roddys and Leahys and Simmonses). And as we went on, we ended up talking about the book *Ancestors.* He said he hadn't really known he would write such a thing, but that once begun, he rather loved going over it all. Finding out the history. And there is such wonderful respect in the writing for all the Middle Western simplicity and religiosity from which his people came. And his family history turns out to be, as of course it would, American history: the history not only of his people but of the development of the Disciples of Christ as a denomination all its own and of the passages of those who made that journey—this delivered in a wonderful, airy, loving, appreciative prose, that I'm finding, again, of course, reads exactly as if one is with him and listening to him talk. Take this small passage, for instance:

> Because I was familiar with the inside of the Christian Church in Lincoln, I thought I understood the form of worship practiced there. It turned out that I had almost everything wrong. Surprised to find that it was not something that sprang from the mind of some narrow-minded Scottish Calvinist, that it was not even Scottish and certainly not Calvinist, I went on, and then on, and on, drawn by the excitement and pleasure of what I found. If the telescope is focused properly, ideas are caught in it as well as people. And people do not have sawdust in their heads but, more often than not, passionate convictions, the strangest and most passionate being what they believe the Lord of the Universe expects of them.

The whole book is studded with this confiding—and, one has to say, *joyful*—tone, the tone of a man who is quite happy to be doing precisely what he is doing. About the early evangelist Barton Warren Stone, he writes a line that I believe best expresses the nature of William Maxwell's prose: "He was like a house with all the doors and windows thrown wide open." That is the sense one has reading him—the sense of a kind of openness and freshness of thought and observation, wedded to prodigious powers of intellection and grace.

That night at the theater in New York, there were several very high-profile entertainment people present— Jules Feiffer, Andre Gregory, Judy Collins, Wallace Shawn, Bob Balaban, and his wife, Lynn Grossman, among them. I walked in there with William and Emily Maxwell.

Annabel Davis-Goff

Reading *War and Peace* to
William Maxwell

IN THE LATE spring of the year 2000, William Maxwell's eyesight began to fail. He was ninety-one years old and as insubstantial as tissue paper. Even his voice had begun to disappear, and often I would have to ask him to repeat what he had said. Sometimes, with embarrassment, twice. Only his mind, with its cool intelligence, and his pleasure in beauty and language, his ability to define and summarize the less than complete ideas I sometimes attempted when I was with him, continued to be as strong as they ever had been.

Bill had stopped writing some time before. First he stopped writing fiction; he said he had written all the stories he'd had and now he was finished. For a little time afterward, he wrote short pieces of nonfiction, taking his time over them: an introduction, an article, a review. In an article, one of a series about being old, for *The New York Times Magazine,* he wrote: "I seem to have lost touch with the place that stories and novels come from. I have no idea why. I still like making sentences."

A little before the *New York Times Magazine* piece, Bill wrote an introduction to *The Springs of Affection,* a collection of short stories by Maeve Brennan. Bill and Maeve Brennan had been friends at *The New Yorker* and he had been her editor. In the introduction he describes how much fun it was until Mr. Shawn decided the level of hilarity caused by having Bill, Brendan Gill, and Maeve close together was bad for morale, and Maeve was moved to the other side of the building.

The Springs of Affection is a collection of wonderful and affecting stories. Many are set in Ranelagh, which Bill describes as a suburb of Dublin, and it may then have been. It is close to where my mother lived in Rathmines; both Ranelagh and Rathmines are now part of the city, although the houses are often freestanding and have a garden behind them. Ranelagh is the better address of the two.

After he had stopped writing fiction, Bill for some time worked on a long essay about Robert Louis Stevenson—he admired Stevenson and was interested in his life—and a form of this essay appeared in *The New Yorker* as a review of the first two volumes of *The Letters of Robert Louis Stevenson.*

"Review" is not quite the right word; Bill wrote essays about books. Literature rather than literary criticism. Or perhaps this is what literary criticism, at its best, is. *The Outermost Dream,* a collection of these essays, is one of my favorites among his books. Another is *Ancestors,* and it seems to me now that when he and I talked our conversation more often drifted around his nonfiction than it did to his stories or novels. We talked about books, and often about our families and childhoods. He would ask about my parents and about my early life in Ireland as part of the first generation born after Irish independence. Bill told me that almost the only subject of disagreement between him and Maeve Brennan was her refusal to read Elizabeth Bowen. On political grounds: since Elizabeth Bowen was (as I am) Anglo-Irish. Maeve's father had fought in the Easter Rising of 1916 and on the Republican side during the Irish Civil War of 1922–23. Frank O'Connor, another friend Bill edited, had also fought with the Republicans. Bill was vague about Irish history but not about the nuances of Irish daily life.

After the Stevenson essay, Bill thought briefly that he would like, with the help of a Russian speaker, to translate something by Turgenev. *A Sportsman's Notebook* was one of Bill's favourites. For a week or two Bill was enthusiastic about the prospect of a translation; then he said he wasn't strong enough. I think that perhaps this was the moment when he realized he was losing his eyesight, and he may have sensed that he would not live long enough to finish the work. Emmy, his wife, was by then sick with the cancer she would bear with a quiet courage that was almost shocking to see, and which would soon kill her. Bill was not much interested in surviving Emmy. She was thirteen years younger than he was, and for a time each struggled to stay alive for the other.

Some time after he stopped writing, and after he had—to use an old-fashioned phrase—put his papers in order, reading became difficult for Bill. He was not now strong enough to hold up a large book and I would sometimes come into the apartment and find him leaning over the coffee table trying to read the *TLS*—one of the few publications he still read—with a magnifying glass. In his *New York Times Magazine* piece, Bill made six allusions to pleasure: reading accounted for two. He wrote "I would read all day long and well into the night if there were no other claims on my time." The others are Emmy's presence, sleeping and dreaming, remembering (his daughters, particularly), and standing and looking hard at everything.

A week or so before we made the arrangement that I should come regularly to read to him, Shirley Steegmuller—the novelist Shirley Hazzard—had come to tea with Bill and Emmy and the subject had turned to *War and Peace*. Bill mentioned that he hadn't read it for some time and, when Emmy went to look for it, it turned out that the Maxwells' copy was at their house in Yorktown Heights. A pretty small house with a lovely garden where in happier times we had gathered each August to celebrate Bill's birthday. I remember long festive lunches and summer afternoons out of doors or in Emmy's studio; the garden full of flowers and the day, it seemed, always sunny; Genji, the Maxwells' greatly indulged cat, lying on Bill's knee or on the lawn under the bird-feeder; the table on which Emmy would have put small flowers from the garden in little jugs and vases. It was unlikely that either Bill or Emmy would ever see the house again. Shirley brought over a paperback edition of *War and Peace*—light enough at that time for Bill to be able to hold—and he started to reread it. He used to say it gave him great comfort.

When he was about a third of the way through the book, Bill told me he could no longer see well enough to read, and I asked if he would like me to read aloud to him. I read for about an hour the first day and when I left I said I would be happy to come back as often as he would like. But it was Emmy who looked after the engagement book and, since she was ill, it was about ten days before it was established that—unless I was told not to—I would come every afternoon at four o'clock to read *War and Peace* to Bill.

During those weeks I watched two people I loved dying, and it made every moment I spent with them infinitely valuable. Each day I would arrive and step quietly into the quiet apartment, the door no longer locked since many people now came and went; the doorbell unrung, since Emmy might be enjoying the reprieve of sleep. I don't remember often being sad, and only wept once. I was comforted by Brookie, the Maxwells' younger daughter, and I was very much aware as I struggled to control myself that it was her parents, not mine, who were dying. Bill and Emmy Maxwell took for me—

as they did for many others—the place of a dead, absent, or unsatisfactory family.

Bill would usually be sitting in the large light room that looked out over the most easterly part of Eighty-sixth Street. The windows of the living room faced north and on the sills were assorted plants. A bougainvillea of some age bloomed that summer, the dead leaves of the winter still attached to the vine. An orchid or two, and other plants I no longer recollect. Across from the apartment was Henderson Place—a few houses and a short narrow cul-de-sac—a small oasis of New York roof planting, and, beyond, the bridge. In *Over By the River,* there is a description of the bridge at night: "The Hell Gate section of the Triborough Bridge was a necklace of sickly-green incandescent pearls."

Over By the River describes this small area of the city, but the view is not the one George Carrington saw from his apartment. ("From our living room," he said, "you can see all the way to the North Pole.") The story, written in 1974, describes the Gracie Square apartment, several blocks away, where the Maxwells lived before they moved to Eighty-sixth Street. In one scene, sadder now than when it was written, George Carrington, taking the family dog for a walk, thinks, as he watches a tanker heading down the river to the ocean, that there are places he would never see, important experiences he would never have: "He might die without ever having heard a nightingale."

Reading *War and Peace* with Bill allowed me a rare and privileged view of how a great writer reads. I had, I suppose, known that anyone who writes above a certain level must read differently from most of us. Nabokov, in the introduction to his *Lectures on Literature,* asks what a reader needs in order to read a book properly and he reproduces a multiple-choice quiz that he offered at "a remote provincial college through which I happened to be jogging on a protracted lecture tour." This is not one of his finer moments but I imagine he was often tired and discouraged. His four correct answers: imagination, memory, a dictionary, and some artistic sense.

I realize now that I don't know what Bill thought of Nabokov, although I know that when he edited his stories at *The New Yorker,* the letters that Nabokov sent to Bill often were decorated with a beautiful hand-drawn butterfly. I know too that Bill didn't completely share Nabokov's feelings about Dostoevsky. When I told Bill I couldn't read Dostoevsky I might have been more circumspect about my opinion without Nabokov's stance to back me up. But Bill just smiled and described a moment he particularly admired in *The Brothers Karamazov*— someone kneeling to beg his valet's pardon. So I don't know what he really thought of Dostoevsky either. We usually agreed on writers and books, in part because if he thought differently from me it was reason enough for me to consider what I thought very carefully. Occasionally we just disagreed. He, for instance, refused to share my admiration for Anthony Powell.

As we read, I began to understand that Bill's own writerly ability and imagination lifted him far above my Nabokovian approach. Or perhaps he was one of the few who could to the full extent read the scenes as Tolstoy had written them. It is not that the book fails to make me weep, or does not horrify me, or that I do not care about the fates of the main characters, but I could not take myself so far into the lives of the Rostovs, or the tensions of the household at Bald Hills, as Bill was able to. Since Bill died I have reread *War and Peace* with the added pleasure and sadness of remembered conversations about certain passages or discussions of details—usually military—that had puzzled us. But it was from another writer that I gained, for a moment, a glimpse of what it might be like to be Bill and to be reading Tolstoy. Not surprisingly, I came across it in *The Outermost Dream*. In it, Bill quotes from a letter by Sylvia Townsend Warner on the subject of Crabbe, the poet, "I read him *as though I were writing him*." In the same book, I also came across a sentence from *War and Peace* quoted by Bill to explain why he would find it difficult to review fiction: "The house was full of that poetic atmosphere of dullness and silence which always accompanies the presence of an engaged couple." It is the sort of thing, Bill wrote, that will keep any reader from escaping out the side door.

Bill and Tolstoy were not, of course, similar, nor is an attempt to suggest that they were a particularly interesting one. But there are, nonetheless, similarities (similarities that perhaps exist among most, perhaps all, good writers) that as we read I began to understand. Tolstoy had chosen as his subject the invasion of Russia, the turning tide of a huge European war, the lives of two families, and that of an awkward but sympathetic young man at the time of the war. Bill chose a small town in the Midwest. Twentieth-century American middle class rather than Russian nineteenth-century aristocracy; Lincoln, Illinois, rather than Moscow and St. Petersburg. The most significant event in Bill's life and work, one which changed him forever and which I think is always present—sometimes only as a ghost in the background—was the death of his mother during the influenza epidemic in 1918. Suddenly and with no warning gone, and with her the end of a safe, happy, conventional childhood. The influenza epidemic was to Bill what Napoleon's Russian campaign was to Tolstoy. In *They Came Like Swallows* and all Bill's largely autobiographical work, the epidemic and the loss of his mother are in the essence of the subject; in other stories and novels they are present as the shadow of loss and aloneness. But for both men, the events themselves are not what most concern them; it is the effect on the characters they describe. After Bill died, I came upon the following passage in *The Outermost Dream*:

> If orphaned children were allowed to deal with their grief in an otherwise unchanged world, they would probably, in time, extricate themselves from it naturally, because of their age. But the circumstances always *are* changed, and it is the constant comparison of the way things are with the way things used to be that sometimes fixes them forever in an attitude of loss.

In the introduction to the translation I read to Bill, Rosemary Edmunds writes that Tolstoy believes that Napoleon was defeated by simplicity, goodness, and truth. Qualities that Bill describes again and again in his work, as he does the redeeming nature of love. Where the two writers part dramatically is in the understanding of the value of art and writing. Toward the end of his life Tolstoy abandoned, or tried to abandon—fortunately for us not always successfully—writing since he thought it took him away from his god; Bill understood that they were the same thing.

We read *War and Peace* not so much to know what life was like in Russia at that moment in history, but to know what we ourselves are like. It is not a book one wishes one were reading for the first time. I read it first when I was thirteen or fourteen, most interested in Natasha and Prince Andrei, Mademoiselle Bourienne; the military part I found, not surprisingly, less exciting. (Bill had last read *War and Peace* in 1986, as I discovered recently when Michael Collier found a postcard Bill had sent from Yorktown Heights in June of that year which reads, in part: "my spare time is divided between gardening and rereading *War and Peace* after 50 years.") Each time I read it I am more taken by the descriptions of war, and of course the reactions and feelings of the men engaged in battle. Bill was interested in the military details, and we would pause sometimes to make sure we both understood what was happening during some of the more complicated descriptions.

Bill's reaction to moments of great beauty, sadness, or

emotion fascinated me. I was born and brought up in Southern Ireland, in a culture where most feeling was kept below the surface, invisible, and, as far as possible, unexperienced. Not entirely connected to this upbringing is my distaste for—and vulnerability to—sentimentality; the combination makes me uncomfortable and inhibited around sentiment. Bill was, more than any serious person I have ever known, open to sentiment. He and I shared a great regard for a play called *The Steward of Christendom* by Sebastian Barry. There is a scene at the end when the young Irish soldier slain in the First World War returns in a dream or vision to his father, who is dying in an asylum. The boy lies beside him on his cot; in life they had not been close. It is a scene I could at first hardly bear to think about, but Bill was to return to it again and again. He and Emmy liked to go to the theatre, although by then it was not possible for either of them, and I gave him a copy of Tom Stoppard's *The Invention of Love* after I had seen the play in London. He wrote to me afterward, mentioning in particular Housman's cri de coeur, "Oh, Mo! Mo! I would have died for you, but I never had the luck!"

Bill was so devoid of sentimentality—that cheap emotion whose reverse side is cruelty—and so essentially hard-minded that he could pause uninhibitedly at these moments of sentiment. He was known all his life for the lack of shame or inhibition with which he would allow his eyes to fill with tears when he read something beautiful or sad. The death of Petya, of Prince Andrei; courage, fear, pain, and loss. And not only in war do the young, beautiful, and privileged die horribly and far from home. The fate of the little princess in her father-in-law's house is as horrible. Bill, the master of the small and sometimes revisited canvas, took Tolstoy's families very much to heart.

Bill's hard-mindedness was a surprise and a pleasure. He was kind, gentle, generous, modest, dignified, and thoughtful. The last quality in a particularly wide sense. He would often say something—always in the same sure quiet way that he wrote—that would untangle a problem, make a decision, remove a doubt. He told me that he wrote with the assumption that if a subject interested him there would be enough readers who would also be interested. He once answered a question of mine with "fancy has a logic of its own." (He also told me that every writer has a lifetime ration of three exclamation points.) It would be hard to overestimate how much difference these observations, and a few others that I selfishly hoard, have made. So it was with surprise and pleasure that one would hear him say no. No to a book, to an idea, to a person. And the no was adamant, definitive, final. One never had the sense that love, to which he gave an even greater value than do most of us, interfered with his critical ability or his judgment of character. He never debased his own currency. Like Tolstoy, he knew it is as necessary in life as it is in art to know the truth. He believed in love, but not in God. In family, friends, and books, not in an afterlife. We would occasionally talk about the possibility of the existence of some higher being, but it was with the same unweighted curiosity with which we would discuss the possibility of life on other planets, agreeing in conclusion on the improbability of any of the theories or beliefs we had discussed. Pierre's spiritual quest—although I am sympathetic to what lies behind it—is not for me one of the more interesting or appealing parts of *War and Peace*. I don't remember Bill ever commenting on it.

There were scenes and moments in the book that we would talk about. Usually when we paused for tea. When I first came to read, Bill would eat a slice of cake with his Hu-Kwa tea. But later, he had difficulty eating more than a morsel at a time and Emmy, who would sometimes lie on the chaise longue, listening with closed eyes, supported by cushions and with a blanket over her legs, could not, toward the end, even drink tea.

Bill was very much affected by Prince Bolkonsky's death. It was one of the places we paused to talk. The mounting tension of the scenes at Bald Hills he admired as much as those in any other sequence in the novel. The plain and frightened Princess Maria; the Prince, her impatient, unkind, and often cruel father; Mademoiselle Bourienne, treacherous and self-serving, but not completely unsympathetic until she has her moment of power; the Prince's quarrels with his daughter and Prince Andrei; and then as the Prince approaches death, angry, unhappy, roaming his house at night with his valet, looking for a place where he can bear to sleep. The loss of his strength, the deterioration of his body, and his eventual helplessness are painfully described. Bill listened to them coolly, admiringly. What he was waiting for was the moment when the Prince, his speech distorted by his stroke, struggles to tell his daughter that he loves her. For Bill the scenes were about love.

There are sequences in *War and Peace* so affecting that one can hardly bear to read them. Petya's death; Natasha sacrificing Prince Andrei as she falls in love with the worthless Kuragin; Nikolai Rostov losing a fortune playing faro with Dolohov. These scenes horrify me every time I think about them. To read them aloud to someone of Bill's sensibility made it possible for me to appreciate their full power. We watched the household goods of the Rostov family unpacked to transport the wounded soldiers, among them (we know it, although the Rostovs do not) the dying Prince Andrei; we crept out the side door with Natasha as she goes to find Andrei and to be forgiven; we followed Pierre to the front. When we read of Pierre's arrival at Borodino and his meeting Boris, who advises him where to position himself to ensure a good view of the battle, I remembered that my grandfather had, during the First World War, in order to see what was happening and to lend a hand, driven with his chauffeur to the front. The umbrella stand by the front door in the house where I grew up was made of a shell casing he brought back.

Usually, just before six o'clock, we would stop reading. Bill was often tired by then and it was close to the time his evening meal would be ready. If we had finished a chapter or were approaching a particularly poignant scene, we would sometimes stop a few minutes early. One afternoon, as we came close to the end of the book, I asked him if he had heard enough for that afternoon and he answered, "Yes, let Petya live one more day." Bill was very much affected by the death of Petya; more forgiving than I of the thoughtlessness of his youth. The boy is not for me one of the more sympathetic characters.

Although we finished the book, we did not finish the epilogue. I had thought, superstitiously, that Bill would not die while we were still reading, and as we came in sight of the end, I tentatively suggested that we might next read *Anna Karenina*. But he smiled and shook his head. The last scene that Bill found more than usually affecting was the one in which Prince Andrei's son, Nikolai, is listening to a conversation between Pierre and Nikolai Rostov, who is now married to the boy's aunt. Nikolai becomes so excited by the conversation that he breaks the quill pens and sealing wax on his uncle's desk. In my copy of *War and Peace,* there is a bookmark several pages farther on.

Two days before he died, I sat with him. Emmy had died six days before and Bill's hold on life had loosened. He had spent much of the day saying good-bye to the friends that his daughter Kate, who had nursed both him and Emmy with calm practical courage, brought in to see him. The moment for reading was past; Bill was by then so weak that I just sat beside his bed and held his hand. Occasionally, he spoke. His voice was little more than a breath—he talked about his mother, about the trees outside their house in Lincoln, about reading in their shade when he was a child. He wondered a little about his mother and her friends, what they had talked about, how they had helped one another. It was like the ghost of a small story. The stories that he wrote that kept his mother and that child and a happy time from being lost. He succeeded with the minimum of words in recalling perfectly a happy moment of his childhood. So that it should not be lost. As his mother is not lost; through his writing he immortalized her.

At Bill and Emmy's memorial service I read the passage where Prince Andrei's regiment, after Smolensk, passes Bald Hills and he rides up to the house where he was born and had spent his childhood. His father and sister have already left; Napoleon's army is only days away. Soon the house and estate will be plundered by the enemy; already Russian regiments, camping overnight, have caused destruction. He rides past a peasant plaiting a bast shoe, and animals that have strayed through broken fences grazing among the rose bushes. He watches two little girls taking green plums from the hothouse. Later, rejoining his regiment, he sees the soldiers, the battle of Borodino still ahead of them, white and naked, laughing and splashing in the muddy lake. "'Flesh, bodies, *chair à canon!*' he reflected, looking at his own naked body and shuddering." It is a scene Prince Andrei remembers in the hospital tent as he lies waiting for the surgeon. The wound will, later, kill Prince Andrei, but after the operation there is a respite from the pain:

After the agony he had borne Prince Andrei was conscious of a well-being such as he had not experienced for a long time. His imagination reverted to all the best and happiest moments of his life, especially his earliest childhood when he used to be undressed and put to bed, when his nurse had sung lullabies over him, and burying his head in the pillows he had felt happy in the mere feeling of being alive.

Edward Hirsch

Portrait of the Artist as an Old Man

1. Meeting

It startles me to realize that William Maxwell was already an old man when I fell in love with him. I looked into his slightly sunken, radiant face, which seemed transparent to me, and suddenly felt overwhelmed by his actual presence, his odd vulnerability. I had been reading him for years, and yet I wasn't really prepared for the person opening up in front of me. Whatever he felt seemed instantly visible in his lined, paper-thin face, some of which had been carved away by surgery. He was like an X-ray held up and exposed to the light. You could see through him.

We came together over a shared admiration for the poet William Meredith. William had suffered a stroke some years before, and a number of his friends and admirers got together in a little theater to read his work aloud. It was a poignant occasion. Mr. Maxwell was one of the last to recite. He was in his late seventies, and when he stood at the podium I was startled by how fragile he looked, how disconcertingly thin. He had an intimate, slightly quavering voice, which also had something steely in it. He was someone who could not be deterred. He swayed a bit as he talked, and the years—the decades—fell away from him. He was a rapturist. He said, "Listening to William Meredith's poems being read aloud, I felt as if I could die with happiness."

At the dinner after the reading, I glued myself to his side. I was not the only one distracted by his wife Emmy's natural beauty. It must have been that way her entire life. Other people entered the conversation; people came and went. He said things that startled me. He said that when he first read Yeats's early poetry he felt as if fairy dust had been sprinkled on him. He said that in college he had written poetry that was of no consequence. He said that he couldn't enjoy the work of any novelist (Trollope, for example) who didn't have some degree of the poet in him.

Poets had figured into his life. He remembered that when he first met Robert Fitzgerald he had driven him up the wall by praising the plays of J. M. Barrie. Fitzgerald was still an undergraduate at Harvard—Maxwell was a graduate student—but he had been introduced to modernism by Dudley Fitts and took a more advanced position. Fitzgerald got him to give up Galsworthy, introduced him to "The Waste Land," and taught him that literature is "serious business." He also spoke of Louise Bogan. Both had a profound effect on him, and he couldn't bear it that they had passed away. He was not reconciled. "People die and they're gone," he said. "I'll never get used to it."

I had never met anyone, let alone an old man, who seemed so emotionally present. It went against the grain of my experience to find someone who had not been stopped or closed up, who had not been defeated by old age. One knew that he had been an editor at *The New Yorker* for forty years, where he had worked with O'Connor, Welty, Salinger, Nabokov, Cheever, Gallant, Updike, Woiwode, and innumerable others, a distinction that he wore lightly, like his pale green seersucker suit. He was modest and incisive. He had an unassuming urbanity mixed with a strange forthrightness. What surprised me was that one could see directly through to the child in him, the rail-thin kid from Lincoln, Illinois, the heartbroken boy who had lost his mother and never got over it—he stubbornly refused to—but also the novelist of childhood, of a lost Midwestern world.

After dinner, the Maxwells and I rode across town in a cab together. It was understood we would become friends. The gift of his attention seemed inexplicable, but real. I can still remember the sound of the cab door slamming in front of his apartment building on the Upper East Side, over by the river. He bounded out with alarming speed, like someone half his age. "Good night," he shouted through the open window, and disappeared.

Good night? I was so magnetized by the quality of his affections that I could scarcely sleep at all. It took me a few more hours to remember something apropos that he had written about Sylvia Townsend Warner's initial visit to *The New Yorker* in 1939. He said, "Her conversation was so enchanting that it made my head swim. I did not want to let her out of my sight. Ever."

2. *Story of Friendship*

I must have written him an excited letter, because he wrote back and said that it allowed us "to dispense with the five or ten years it takes people to become friends when they leave it to circumstance." He also spoke of Meredith's heart-stopping recital of his own poems ("I felt I was pushing a wheelbarrow over Niagara blindfolded, until he got the last word out") and of the poet who had unexpectedly leaned over to him in the auditorium and said, "I can't tell you how many times in my life I have been Lymie Peters," whereupon he pulled out a copy of *The Folded Leaf* for an autograph. Maxwell was astonished. "I was only Lymie Peters once," he confessed, "and I don't dare think what it could have been to repeat and repeat the experience."

Our friendship feels as if it happened all at once, as if it arrived full-blown, but of course it didn't. There were stages. The chronology confuses me a little, or maybe it doesn't seem that important. I remember the

Edward Hirsch ~ 191

letter in which he enclosed his phone number and the first time he called to praise something I had written. I remember a high-spirited dinner party with the Wilkinsons and the Colliers. Bill said that he wished it were like an egg timer so that he could turn it upside down and begin all over again, at any time he liked. It was the way life ought to be.

My initial visit to the Maxwells in their apartment on Eighty-sixth and East End set the pattern. I came on time and stayed too long. I had trouble tearing myself away. We sat in the living room, which was austere and spacious. We drank tea from china cups and nibbled cookies. Emmy visited for a while and drifted off. I pulled things down from the walnut bookcases. We stood at the large windows in the far corner of the room and gazed at the street, eight floors below. We sat next to each other on the couch and talked about books (we had both been befriended by books when we were young) and childhood, our irrepressible first subject.

It's hard to describe the exact character—the quality—of Maxwell's attention. It was undivided. It was disarmingly frank. He asked you all about your childhood, which he marveled at, and gave freely of his own. He talked about growing up in a small town, about the way the houses set back calmly from the wide streets and the elms cast a pattern of light and shade on the pavement. People didn't lock their doors at night and their faces were filled with kindness. He believed that only a few things had happened to him in his life, but some of them he had felt deeply.

It didn't take long to discover that when he talked about the past, it was vividly, even painfully, present to him. It was as if at any moment he could close his eyes and slip through a thin membrane in time. He didn't need a *petite madeleine* to send him there. I once asked him if he missed the past. He looked at me with some surprise and replied that he didn't miss the past because he was never separated from it. He said, "I have a huge set of memories, which I carry around like a packed suitcase."

Maxwell's past was so immediate to him because there was such a clear Before and After in his life, which was sundered in two by the death of his mother. Everything was fastened at a specific moment in time when his childhood was lost forever. That's when he discovered what he called, in a resonant phrase, "the fragility of human happiness." I have the harrowing image of him as a ten-year-old boy pacing up and down the floor of an empty house at night with his father, both of them in bewildered mourning, in numb grief, unable to comfort each other. His fate was sealed on those nights. There's a telling moment near the end of *So Long, See You Tomorrow* when the narrator is talking to his psychiatrist about his mother's death. He means to say, "I couldn't bear it," but what comes out of his mouth is "I can't bear it," and then he rushes into the city in tears. He says, "New York City is a place where one can weep on the sidewalk in perfect privacy." There is something Maxwellian about inconsolable grief. The loss of his mother was so traumatic and intolerable for him that his memory, supplemented by imagination, set out to defy it.

I first felt the inconsolable nature of Maxwell's work when I read his second novel, *They Came Like Swallows,* a book that has left me in tears more than once. One of the early reviews called it "heartwarming," a common opinion about his work, which grates on me because it misses the mark. On the contrary, I find his work intensely sad and quietly heartbroken. It is very American. The surface is calm, the sentences poised and deceptively offhanded, but what drives them is a desperate need to hold on to a world irrevocably gone. At one point I asked him—I suspect it was because I liked the form—where he had written the three sections of the novel. He copied out his answer in my edition of the book: "The first section was written over a year at a farmhouse in Wisconsin. Part 2 in a summer at the MacDowell Colony where Robert Fitzgerald was translating, I think, *The Alcestis* of Euripides. Part 3 was written in two weeks in an old house in Urbana, Illinois, walking the floor and in tears."

Grief had a deep hold on him, and yet I have seldom known anyone who took such deep interest in the inner lives of his friends. His sympathy seemed boundless for both books and friends. "To be up to the eyebrows in a great work of literature is such happiness," he wrote to me once. "I remember crying in Greek over the death of Socrates."

It's hard to write about your friends, as Bill once told me when he was trying to write an obituary piece about

Francis Steegmuller, whom he had known for fifty years. "If you write too fondly it comes out mush, and if you aren't careful they become a character in a story, which is inappropriate."

Maxwell wasn't a wisdom machine, or a figure in a story. Yet it strikes me as a triumph of character that someone who suffered such early sorrow later developed such a capacity for friendship, for shared happiness. Sometimes, when you asked him a question, he closed his eyes for a long time and drifted off—where was he going?—but when he came back he gave an irresistibly truthful answer. It was as if he had let you into his daydreaming process. He seems never to have resisted a generous impulse. We were giddy in each other's presence. We suffered from all we had to say to each other.

Time had a way of stopping when you were in his presence. Eventually, it was necessary to leave. I always felt dazed after one of our marathon visits. I had been seduced all over again. I am surely not the only one who came away from his apartment feeling that I was loved in excess of my actual worth. Every visit felt like a last one, which was part of its mystique. We had ten years of friendship, yet our mutual happiness in each other's presence was tinged with the inevitable sadness of parting.

3. Interview in Yorktown Heights

I never worked with Maxwell as an editor, but I did get a taste of how he worked when I was commissioned to write a piece about him for *DoubleTake* magazine. I was daunted by the thought of writing about each one of his books in turn, and so I procrastinated endlessly writing the piece. Finally, I confessed my dilemma to him. He wrote back: "My life seems to me a subject too thoroughly (if anything) dealt with in one place or another. The books I don't have any ideas about. I just did them. But it occurs to me that we might have a conversation about old age and what it is like to be aware that your days are numbered. That may interest you. I don't know what I think about these two things and would be interested to find out." He went on to suggest that I could hang the piece on an occasion, like his birthday party. It was a perfect (and practical) solution. Thus Maxwell not only became the subject of my piece; he also taught me how to conceptualize and write it.

One August morning in the summer of 1996, I caught an early morning train from Manhattan to Croton-Harmon. Emmy met me. At seventy-five, she was still a radiant presence, utterly charmed and charming, preternaturally gracious, though there was also something coltish in her, something wild just under the surface. Her dark brown eyes always seemed unusually wide open, wide apart. They were filled with light. She was a Westerner with a spiritual side. Her favorite song was "Don't Fence Me In." It was hard not to want to linger in her presence. We took our time. We drove through a couple of picturesque villages, meandered off to admire a local waterfall, and traveled down various country lanes before turning into the gravel driveway of the house on Baptist Church Road, where Bill came rushing out of the house.

I liked coming out to their country place, a tiny pre-fab house that arrived in Westchester on a flatbed truck sometime in the early 1920s. Bill had bought it for about five thousand dollars in the early 1940s, before he was married. Over the years, the Maxwells enclosed the front porch and converted it into Bill's study, built a freestanding screened-in gazebo, and built a studio for Emmy, who was a painter. Bill was mad for flowers, and as we drove up to the house I could see the grounds covered with large patches of color. I carried my suitcase into the house, settled into the guest room, and then went looking for Bill again, who had disap-peared. "Oh, he's already in the study," Emmy said. "He's ready to work."

Sure enough, Bill was stationed at his desk—a simple sturdy piece of pearwood—in his small study crammed with papers, books, photographs, paintings, records—the accumulation of years. "I am slowly being crowded out by the objects," he told me, "but even more by the associations around the objects."

I noticed photographs of his two daughters, Brookie and Kate; a couple of Emmy's paintings depicting places where they had lived; a postcard of a young man with one hand on his forehead, bent over a piece of paper, lost in thought. Bill called it "a picture of the inner life."

There was an oversize photograph of Colette, a pho-tograph of the Wisconsin novelist Zona Gale—the first writer he ever met and a sort of literary fairy godmother to him ("She had one foot in the mystic camp," he once told me)—and another of Robert Fitzgerald. "I knew he was something I needed, and that he didn't suffer fools gladly," Bill had explained about their first meeting. "I loved him on first sight. He was so difficult, so intransigent, so obviously a true poet."

Over the years Bill had effected his own eccentric way of conducting an interview. I had heard about the ritual many times before, and I was amused to be participating in it. It went like this. I'd lob a question aloud. Bill would take a moment, swivel around on his chair, grab a sheet of blank paper, and then start typing on his old Smith Corona 1200. He had a sort of pecking, rapid-fire method of typing. "All the thoughts are in the typewriter," he told me. I liked watching him work. He'd pause, type, stop, read what he had written, scowl, then start typing again, faster now, following the heartbeat of a thought, the development of an idea. When he was done he peeled off the page and handed it to me, searching my face while I read the answer. If I had a follow-up question he'd take the paper and insert it back into the typewriter. If I had a new question, he'd reel in a new sheet and start firing away. I found it strangely effective—a way of mixing the intimacy of conversation with the precision of writing.

While Bill answered the questions, I snooped around the bookshelves. I found a full set of Chekhov's stories— an obvious model—two shelves of works by Sylvia

Townsend Warner, a couple of shelves of his own books in no particular order, a collection of Welty's photographs (preface by William Maxwell). There were no biographies in his office, but plenty of collections of letters. I found full editions of the letters of Horace Walpole, William James, and Robert Louis Stevenson. There was also *The Happiness of Getting It Down Right,* a collection of his own recent epistolary exchanges with Frank O'Connor.

While our interview was proceeding, the preparations for the party were also going into full swing. A friend of Emmy's arrived to help set things up. The gardener stopped by; someone dropped off wine. The phone rang constantly. Some well-wishers wouldn't be put off, and so Bill was called off to the kitchen. He'd come right back and sit down at his desk. All morning there were the questions of whether or not it would rain (it wouldn't rain on Bill's birthday!) and where the luncheon should take place. It was finally decided to have the lunch in Emmy's air-conditioned studio rather than on the outdoor porch (a good thing, too, since it ended up pouring rain). There was also the question of Harriet's fish. Harriet had sent a salmon from Ireland and it still hadn't arrived. A flurry of international calls turned up that it had been delayed in customs at Kennedy Airport. Listening to the party taking shape all over the house, asking Bill questions and then watching his long hands floating fluidly over the typewriter, I started to feel as if I were participating in a Chekhov story.

4. *Some Things He Said*

I once said to Joe Mitchell that the only part about dying that I minded was that when you are dead you can't read Tolstoy.

. . .

I am no longer surprised at being as old as I am because I went through two or three preliminary shocks that prepared me for it. They all occurred in front of the bathroom mirror while I was shaving. The first was "What am I doing attached to that old man?" The second, a few days later, was "But I don't want to leave the party."

. . .

It isn't so much that time seems mysterious to me as that I wonder if it is necessary.

. . .

There was a time when I was able to feel (even though I knew it was irrational) that they would all be waiting for me when I died—my mother, my Uncle Doc, my aunts Edith and Annette. What that amounts to is that the child expected it, and the man humored him in this idea.

. . .

There was a woman, one of several surrogate mothers, who lived on a farm in Wisconsin, where I went to work when I was eighteen, and which afterward became a second home to me. She was a very vital woman. She lived to be ninety-five or ninety-six, and told her daughter at the end of her life that she was tired, that she had lived long enough. This has been a great comfort to me.

• • •

I did things I shouldn't have but have been on the whole so fortunate that it would seem ungrateful to regret anything. But you haven't asked about my mind. It is beginning to fray. . . . There is slippage in the upper story.

• • •

I used to think that when I got to be an old man I would sit in a wheelchair and drink scotch all day. Now that I am an old man I find I don't like scotch and one glass of red wine at dinner is all I can manage comfortably.

• • •

The energy that it requires to imagine a novel and then carry this idea through to the final page is simply not there anymore. When people ask me, "What are you writing?," even though I know they have asked the question only out of politeness, I want to pick up something and throw it at them. Which must mean some resentment on my part at the diminishment of certain powers that old age inevitably means.

• • •

About kindness. I have taken so much of my emotional "attitudes," if that is the right word, from my mother. When I was a very small child I was out riding with my father and mother one evening after supper and as they were going through town, my father suddenly pulled on the reins and stopped the carriage. A little boy had darted into the street and been run over just ahead of us. He was about my age, and the son of a doctor, and he was carried into his father's office. My father and mother got the carriage and, taking me with them, went into the waiting room. My mother disappeared behind a glass wall and I could tell she was holding the boy and talking to him, saying "Now, now, now, now . . ." Using just the tone of voice she used when I was upset. But it sunk in that anyone in trouble had a claim on her feelings.

On another occasion we were at dinner and the phone rang, and when my mother came back from the telephone she said, "There has been a cyclone in Matoon, and they want people to send food down in a freight car to the station." Whereupon she took all the food off the table, when we had barely started to eat, wrapped it in a cloth and gave it to my father who took it downtown, and I went to bed hungry.

* * *

"Bravely frank!" How can you say such a thing! I am truthful only once in a month of Sundays. And only when I am fairly sure the person can stand it. Mostly people can't, as Eliot said, bear very much reality. If I were to die and go to Heaven, if there were a Heaven, I would go around telling the truth all day long, never mind the angels and their harping.

* * *

When I was a child and would tell my mother, "My

feelings are hurt," I felt that they existed, my feelings, with the solidity of material objects. Because my older brother teased me and nobody could make him stop, I cried at least once a day until he went away to college, after which I didn't cry any more than people normally do. But I listened, in a manner of speaking, to my feelings, and when it was sensible always tried to act on them.

• • •

When I am writing a novel or even a story it is as if I had entered a room and closed the door behind me. The concentration it takes to shape a story, to watch characters emerge and become in the round, to move sentences around a dozen times until they are locked into place usually involves a withdrawal from one's present and exterior life.

• • •

Don't you and the poet live side by side and lie awake with insomnia in the same bed at night?

• • •

I have come to put more faith in what actually happened. I have come to feel that life is the Scheherazade.

• • •

[My sense of my mother's death changed from book to book.] In *They Came Like Swallows* it was pretty much raw grief. In *The Folded Leaf* she is a shadowy figure in the background of Lymie Peters. I don't remember if it is in the novel or not, but when, in actual life, I did cut my throat with the intention to die, it was also with the expectation that I would join my mother.

The woman in *Time Will Darken It* is not drawn from her, though she lived in my mother's house.

In *So Long, See You Tomorrow* I wasn't so much writing about her (although I did briefly) as her absence. But perhaps emotionally speaking there is no difference.

In *Ancestors* the chapters about the happiness of our family life was a kind of testifying. It was also like painting. As if years and habits and feelings could also be made visual. But it is done, I think, from a distance and with acceptance.

By the time I came to write the two stories about the black people, Billie Dyer and his sister who was my mother's housekeeper, I tried to abandon the child's viewpoint and see my mother as an adult would have. Allowing her to be less than perfect, but at the same time, with no withdrawal of love. More as if I had become Isherwood's camera and were photographing her in this or that moment.

But also, I wrote less about how she was, what she meant to me, and more about what she was and meant to other people.

When I was in analysis I wrote a full-length play which I told to Theodore Reik, lying on the couch. My mother arrived at a mysterious airport, having managed a return to life in this world. Only to find that my father had remarried and didn't need her. That I was on the point of marrying, and if she stayed

I would be torn between my love for her and my love for the young woman I was about to marry. Feeling that there was no longer any place for her, that life had closed over and she was shut out, she returned to the airport. The curtain line was the "I" character saying to his fiancée, "Hold me!"

Whether you want to or meant to or not, in old age you find yourself thinking whatever is simply is and must be accepted. I suppose the child goes on grieving. The man—

• • •

What life resembles sometimes, though fortunately not too often, is a jack-in-the-box.

• • •

My own part I would be more satisfied with if I had said that Emmy has kept my body and soul together for more than fifty years, that I never tire of looking at her face, that if I hadn't married her I wouldn't have married anybody and so wouldn't have been able to write about a life that was in any way whole.

5. Dying

*Old age is what you make of it, and what
old age makes of you.*

What he made of his circumstance, and what it made of him, turned him into the most lovable person I've ever known. I once asked him how he managed it. He said that in his thirties he was terribly alone and that he decided that he wanted to be loved more than anything else. The way to do that was to love other people unreservedly. He said, "I saw people all around me, saw what they were like, understood what they were going through, and without waiting for them to love me, loved them."

It worked beyond measure. It never failed to surprise him, even at the very end of his life, that so many people loved him so completely. During the last few weeks of their lives, when Emmy was dying of cancer and Bill was declining rapidly from old age, I would sometimes stop over just to be near them. I was one of the circle, all of us inconsolable. The week before he died I confessed that I didn't think I could stand it without him, and he said to me, "I've lived with death my whole life, and I know that the people we love we carry with us always. They're part of us."

His curiosity—his interest in other people—never lagged. For example, he wanted me to see the Chardin show at the Met, which he and Emmy had gotten out of their deathbeds to visit. I was teaching a course on reading poetry for high school teachers, and it was hard to get away during the week. One night I came back to a telephone message from his nurse waiting for me at my hotel. The red light blinked on and off in the dark. "Mr. Maxwell wants to know if you have seen the Chardin show yet."

The day before Emmy died, I was standing behind Bill's wheelchair while he gazed at her face. A group of us were gathered around her hospital bed. She was wearing a Chinese brocade jacket. It was hard to take your eyes off her. Her hair was cropped short, her face thin but luminous. Her eyes were deep brown pools lit from within. "I think of all the men she could have made happy," he lobbed up at me. "All of them poets." She had saved him, as he had said many times, and he never got over his great good fortune at having found her.

Emmy wanted to dispel the sadness. She wanted each of us to take a glass of champagne. The cork popped. We toasted and sang "Don't Fence Me In." Bill held her hand. He whispered and hummed along. Emmy closed her eyes and was ready to slip away. She wanted to hear "Death and the Maiden." One felt that she was going somewhere, that she believed in something on the other side. Each of us said goodnight, good-bye. "This is the hardest thing I've ever had to do," she whispered to me as I leaned over to kiss her cheek. Her voice was so low that I couldn't tell if I was hearing her right. "Rilke says that each of us must die his own death. Now I have to die mine." And then she was asleep.

In the end, he was waiting for her to die first. It was a final act of love, a last courtesy. The night after Emmy died, I had an irresistible urge to be near him, and so I showed up unannounced at his apartment around 10 P.M. He heard my voice in the hallway and called me into his bedroom. He looked incredibly fragile lying on the bed. "Her hand was warm," he said. He remembered that after his mother died her hand was ice-cold, the touch of a corpse that had stayed with him for eighty years. But he was comforted by the fact that Emmy's hand had retained its warmth for several hours. I kissed him goodnight.

When I was going out the door, he whispered, "Have you seen the Chardin show yet?" I hadn't. I was stunned that he could think of it. I went the next morning—the paintings have a kind of deathly beauty that has haunted me ever since—and then flew right over to his apartment to please him. I told him the only thing missing from the show was that he wasn't there to see it with me. He said, "I *was* there with you."

In the days before Maxwell died, he talked about the lightness of being. He was so thin and bony that one felt as if he could simply float away. He ate a little. He resolved that he would live as long as he could for the sake of his daughters. He said that he had been so lucky in his life that to wish for anything more would be greedy. Unlike his wife, he did not believe in the other side. His religion had been literature. He closed his eyes and said that he liked to think of dying as taking a permanent nap.

I can't reconcile myself to the fact that he is gone. The night before he passed away I stood on the sidewalk outside his apartment building and burst into tears. I was grieving in advance. I couldn't bear to be without him. I still can't. William Maxwell knew something about inconsolable grief. People hurried by on either side of me, but no one even glanced my way. It started to rain. The night opened its arms. New York City is a place where one can weep on the sidewalk in perfect privacy.

William Maxwell

The Writer as Illusionist: A Speech Delivered at Smith College March 4, 1955

One of the standard themes of Chinese painting is the spring festival on the river. I'm sure many of you have seen some version of it. There is one in the Metropolitan Museum. It has three themes woven together: the river, which comes down from the upper right, and the road along the river, and the people on the riverbanks. As the scroll unwinds, there is, first, the early-morning mist on the rice fields and some boys who cannot go to the May Day festival because they have to watch their goats. Then there is a country house, and several people starting out for the city, and a farmer letting water into a field by means of a water wheel, and then more people and buildings—all kinds of people all going toward the city for the festival. And along the riverbank there are various entertainers—a magician, a female tightrope walker, several fortune-tellers, a phrenologist, a man selling spirit money, a man selling patent medicine, a storyteller. I prefer to think that it is with this group—the shoddy entertainers earning their living by the riverbank on May Day—that Mr. Bellow, Mr. Gill, Miss Chase, on the platform, Mr. Ralph Ellison and Mrs. Kazin, in the audience, and I, properly speaking, belong. Writers—narrative writers—are people who perform tricks.

Before I came up here, I took various books down from their shelf and picked out some examples of the kind of thing I mean. Here is one:

"I have just returned this morning from a visit to my landlord—the solitary neighbor that I shall be troubled with . . ."

One of two things—there will be more neighbors turning up than the narrator expects, or else he will very much wish that they had. And the reader is caught; he cannot go away until he finds out which of his two guesses is correct. This is, of course, a trick.

Here is another: *"None of them knew the color of the sky. . . ."* Why not? Because they are at sea, pulling at the oars in an open boat; and so are you.

Here is another trick: *"Call me Ishmael. . . ."* A pair of eyes looking into your eyes. A face. A voice. You have entered into a personal relationship with a stranger, who will perhaps make demands on you, extraordinary personal demands; who will perhaps insist that you love him; who perhaps will love you in a way that is upsetting and uncomfortable.

Here is another trick: *"Thirty or forty years ago, in one of those gray towns along the Burlington railroad, which are so much grayer today than they were then, there was a house well known from Omaha to Denver for its hospitality and for a certain charm of atmosphere . . ."*

A door opens slowly in front of you, and you cannot see who is opening it but, like a sleepwalker, you have to go in.

Another trick: *"It was said that a new person had appeared on the seafront—a lady with a dog . . ."*

The narrator appears to be, in some way, underprivileged, socially. She perhaps has an invalid father that she has to take care of, and so she cannot walk along the promenade as often as she would like. Perhaps she is not asked many places. And so she has not actually set eyes on this interesting new person that everyone is talking about. She is therefore all the more interested. And meanwhile, surprisingly, the reader cannot forget the lady, or the dog, or the seafront.

Here is another trick: *"It is a truth universally acknowledged that a single man in possession of a good fortune must be in want of a wife . . ."*

An attitude of mind, this time. A way of looking at people that is ironical, shrewd, faintly derisive, and that suggests that every other kind of writing is a trick (this is a special trick, in itself) and that this book is going to be about life as it really is, not some fabrication of the author's.

So far as I can see, there is no legitimate sleight of hand involved in practicing the arts of painting, sculpture, and music. They appear to have had their origin in religion, and they are fundamentally serious. In writing—in all writing but especially in narrative writing—you are continually being taken in. The reader, skeptical, experienced, with many demands on his time and many ways of enjoying his leisure, is asked to believe in people he knows don't exist, to be present at scenes that never occurred, to be amused or moved or instructed just as he would be in real life, only the life exists in somebody else's imagination. If, as Mr. T. S. Eliot says, humankind cannot bear very much reality, then that would account for their turning to the charlatans operating along the riverbank—to the fortune-teller, the phrenologist, the man selling spirit money, the storyteller. Or there may be a different explanation; it may be that what humankind cannot bear directly it can bear indirectly, from a safe distance.

The writer has everything in common with the vaudeville magician except this: The writer must be taken in by his own tricks. Otherwise, the audience will begin to yawn and snicker. Having practiced more or less incessantly for five, ten, fifteen, or twenty years, knowing that the trunk has a false bottom and the opera hat a false top, with the white doves in a cage ready to be handed to him from the wings and his clothing full of unusual, deep pockets containing odd playing cards and colored scarves knotted together and not knotted together and the American flag, he must begin by pleasing himself. His mouth must be the first mouth that drops open in surprise, in wonder, as (presto chango!) this character's heartache is dragged squirming from his inside coat pocket, and that character's future has become his past while he was not looking.

With his cuffs turned back, to show that there is no possibility of deception being practiced on the reader, the writer invokes a time: He offers the reader a wheat field on a hot day in July, and a flying machine, and a little boy with his hand in his father's. He has been brought to the wheat field to see a flying machine go up. They stand, waiting, in a crowd of people. It is a time when you couldn't be sure, as you can now, that a flying machine would go up. Hot, tired, and uncomfortable, the little boy wishes they could go home. The wheat field is like an oven. The flying machine does not go up.

The writer will invoke a particular place: With a cardinal and a tourist home and a stretch of green grass and this and that, he will make Richmond, Virginia.

He uses words to invoke his version of the Forest of Arden. If he is a good novelist, you can lean against his trees; they will not give way. If he is a bad novelist, you probably shouldn't. Ideally, you ought to be able to shake them until an apple falls on your head. (The apple of understanding.)

The novelist has tricks of detail. For example, there is Turgenev's hunting dog, in *A Sportsman's Notebook*. The sportsman, tired after a day's shooting, has accepted a ride in a peasant's cart, and is grateful for it. His dog is not. Aware of how foolish he must look as he is being lifted into the cart, the unhappy dog smiles to cover his embarrassment. . . . There is the shop of the live fish, toward the beginning of Malraux's *Man's Fate.* A conspirator goes late at night to a street of pet shops in Shanghai and knocks on the door of a dealer in live fish. They are both involved in a plot to assassinate someone. The only light in the shop is a candle; the fish are asleep in phosphorescent bowls. As the hour that the assassination will be attempted is mentioned, the water on the surface of the bowls begins to stir feebly. The carp, awakened by the sound of voices, begin to swim round and round, and my hair stands on end.

These tricks of detail are not important; they have nothing to do with the plot or the idea of either piece of writing. They are merely exercises in literary virtuosity, but nevertheless in themselves so wonderful that to overlook them is to miss half the pleasure of the performance.

There is also a more general sleight of hand—tricks that involve the whole work, tricks of construction. Nothing that happens in Elizabeth Bowen's *The House in Paris,* none of the characters, is, for me, as interesting as the way in which the whole thing is put together. From that all the best effects, the real beauty of the book, derive.

And finally there are the tricks that involve the projection of human character. In the last book that I have read, Ann Birstein's novel, *The Troublemaker,* there is a girl named Rhoda, who would in some places, at certain periods of the world's history, be considered beautiful, but who is too large to be regarded as beautiful right now. It is time for her to be courted, to be loved— high time, in fact. And she has a suitor, a young man who stops in to see her on his way to the movies alone. There is also a fatality about the timing of these visits; he always comes just when she has washed her hair. She is presented to the reader with a bath towel around her wet head, her hair in pins, in her kimono, sitting on the couch in the living room, silent, while her parents make conversation with the suitor. All her hopes of appearing to advantage lie shattered on the carpet at her feet. She is inconsolable but dignified, a figure of supportable pathos. In the midst of feeling sorry for her you burst out laughing. The laughter is not unkind.

These forms of prestidigitation, these surprises, may not any of them be what makes a novel great, but unless it has some of them, I do not care whether a novel is great or not; I cannot read it.

It would help if you would give what I am now about to read to you only half your attention. It doesn't require any more than that, and if you listen only now and then, you will see better what I am driving at.

Begin with breakfast and the tipping problem.
Begin with the stealing of the marmalade dish and the breakfast tray still there.

The marmalade dish, shaped like a shell, is put on the cabin-class breakfast tray by mistake, this once. It belongs in first class.

Begin with the gate between first and second class.

Begin with the obliging steward unlocking the gate for them.

The gate, and finding their friends who are traveling first class, on the glassed-in deck.

The gate leads to the stealing of the marmalade dish.

If you begin with the breakfast tray, then—no, begin with the gate and finding their friends.

And their friends' little boy, who had talked to Bernard Baruch and asked Robert Sherwood for his autograph.

The couple in cabin class have first-class accommodations for the return voyage, which the girl thinks they are going to exchange, and the man secretly hopes they will not be able to.

But they have no proper clothes. They cannot dress for dinner if they do return first class.

Their friend traveling first class on the way over has brought only one evening dress, which she has to wear night after night.

Her husband tried to get cabin-class accommodations and couldn't.

This is a lie, perhaps.

They can afford the luxury of traveling first class but disapprove of it.

They prefer to live more modestly than they need to.

They refuse to let themselves enjoy, let alone be swept off their feet by, the splendor and space.

But they are pleased that their little boy, aged nine, has struck up a friendship with Bernard Baruch and Robert Sherwood.

They were afraid he would be bored on the voyage.

Also, they themselves would never have dared approach either of these eminent figures, and are amazed that they have begotten a child with courage.

The girl is aware that her husband has a love of luxury and is enjoying the splendor and space they haven't paid for.

On their way back to the barrier, they encounter Bernard Baruch.

His smile comes to rest on them, like the beam from a lighthouse, and then after a few seconds passes on.

They discover that they are not the only ones who have been exploring.

Their table companions have all found the gate.

When the steward unlocked the gate for the man and the girl, he let loose a flood.

The entire cabin class has spread out in both directions, into tourist as well as first class.

Begin with the stealing of the marmalade dish.

The man is ashamed of his conscientiousness but worried about the stewardess.

Will she have to pay for the missing marmalade dish?

How many people? Three English, two Americans cabin class, three Americans first class.

Then the morning on deck.

The breakfast tray still there, accusing them, before they go up to lunch.

The Orkney Islands in the afternoon.

The movie, which is shown to cabin class in the afternoon, to first class in the evening.

The breakfast tray still in the corridor outside their cabin when they go to join their friends in first class in the bar before dinner.

With her tongue loosened by liquor, the girl confesses her crime.

They go down to the cabin after dinner, and the tray is gone.

In the evening the coast of France, lights, a lighthouse.

The boat as immorality.

The three sets of people.

Begin in the late afternoon with the sighting of the English islands.

Begin with the stealing of the marmalade dish.

No, begin with the gate.

Then the stealing of the marmalade dish.

Then the luncheon table with the discovery that other passengers have been exploring and found the gate between first and second class.

Then the tray accusing them.

What do they feel about stealing?

When has the man stolen something he wanted as badly as the girl wanted that marmalade dish for an ashtray?

From his mother's purse, when he was six years old.

The stewardess looks like his mother.

Ergo, he is uneasy.

They call on their friends in first class one more time, to say goodby, and as they go back to second class, the girl sees, as clearly as if she had been present, that some time during the day her husband has managed to slip away from her and meet the stewardess and pay for the marmalade dish she stole.

And that is why the breakfast tray disappeared.

He will not allow himself, even on shipboard, the splendor and space of an immoral act.

He had to go behind her back and do the proper thing.

A writer struggling—unsuccessfully, as it turned out; the story was never written—to change a pitcher of water into a pitcher of wine.

In *The Listener* for January 27th, 1955, there is a brief but wonderfully accurate description of a similar attempt carried off successfully:

"Yesterday morning I was in despair. You know that bloody book which Dadie and Leonard extort, drop by drop from my breast? Fiction, or some title to that effect. I couldn't screw a word from me; and at last dropped my head in my hands, dipped my pen in the ink, and wrote these words, as if automatically, on a clean sheet: Orlando, a Biography. No sooner had I done this than my body was flooded with rapture and my brain with ideas. I wrote rapidly till twelve . . ."

It is safe to assume that on that wonderful (for us as well as her) morning, the writer took out this word and put in that and paused only long enough to admire the effect; she took—on that morning or others like it—the very words out of this character's mouth in order to give them, unscrupulously, to that character; she annulled marriages and brought dead people back to life when she felt the inconvenience of having to do without them. She cut out the whole last part of the scene she had been working on so happily and feverishly for most of the morning because she saw suddenly that it went past the real effect into something that was just writing. Just writing is when the novelist's hand is not quicker than the reader's eye. She persuaded, she struggled with, she beguiled this or that character that she had made up out of whole cloth (or almost) to speak his mind, to open his heart. Day after day, she wrote till twelve, employing tricks no magician had ever achieved before, and using admirably many that they had, until, after some sixty pages, something quite serious happened. Orlando changed sex—that is, she exchanged the mind of a man for the mind of a woman; this trick was only partly successful—and what had started out as a novel became a brilliant, slaphappy essay. It would have been a great pity—it would have been a real loss if this particular book had never been written; even so, it is disappointing. I am in no position to say what happened, but it seems probable from the writer's diary—fortunately, she kept one—that there were too many interruptions; too many friends invited themselves and their husbands and dogs and children for the weekend.

Though the writer may from time to time entertain paranoiac suspicions about critics and book reviewers, about his publisher, and even about the reading public, the truth is that he has no enemy but interruption. The man from Porlock has put an end to more masterpieces than the Turks—was it the Turks?—did when they set fire to the library at Alexandria. Also, odd as it may seem, every writer has a man from Porlock inside him who gladly and gratefully connives to bring about these interruptions.

If the writer's attention wanders for a second or two, his characters stand and wait politely for it to return to them. If it doesn't return fairly soon, their feelings are hurt and they refuse to say what is on their minds or in their hearts. They may even turn and go away, without explaining or leaving a farewell note or a forwarding address where they can be reached.

But let us suppose that owing to one happy circumstance and another, including the writer's wife, he has a good morning; he has been deeply attentive to the performers and the performance. Suppose that—because this is common practice, I believe—he begins by making a few changes here and there, because what is behind him, all the scenes that come before the scene he is now working on, must be *perfect*, before he can tackle what lies ahead. (This is the most dangerous of all the tricks in the repertoire, and probably it would be wiser if he omitted it from his performance: it is the illusion of illusions, and all a dream. And tomorrow morning, with a clearer head, making a fresh start, he will change back the changes, with one small insert that makes all the difference.) But to continue: Since this is very close work, watch-mender's work, really, this attentiveness, requiring a magnifying glass screwed to his eye and resulting in poor posture, there will probably be, somewhere at the back of his mind, a useful corrective vision, something childlike and simple that represents the task as a whole. He will perhaps see the material of his short story as a pond, into which a stone is tossed, sending out a circular ripple; and then a second stone is tossed into the pond, sending out a second circular ripple that is inside the first and that ultimately overtakes it; and then a third stone; and a fourth; and so on. Or he will see himself crossing a long level plain, chapter after chapter, toward the mountains on the horizon. If there were no mountains, there would be no novel; but they are still a long way away—those scenes of excitement, of the utmost drama, so strange, so sad, that will write themselves; and meanwhile, all the knowledge, all the art, all the imagination at his command will be needed to cover this day's march on perfectly level ground.

As a result of too long and too intense concentration, the novelist sooner or later begins to act peculiarly. During the genesis of his book, particularly, he talks to himself in the street; he smiles knowingly at animals and birds; he offers Adam the apple, for Eve, and with a half involuntary movement of his right arm imitates the writhing of the snake that nobody knows about yet. He spends the greater part of the days of his creation in his bathrobe and slippers, unshaven, his hair uncombed, drinking water to clear his brain, and hardly distinguishable from an inmate in an asylum. Like many such unfortunate people, he has delusions of grandeur. With the cherubim sitting row on row among the constellations, the seraphim in the more expensive seats in the *primum mobile*, waiting, ready, willing to be astonished, to be taken in, the novelist, still in his bathrobe and slippers, with his cuffs rolled back, says *Let there be* (after who knows how much practice beforehand) . . . *Let there be* (and is just as delighted as the angels and the reader and everybody else when there actually is) *Light*.

Not always, of course. Sometimes it doesn't work. But say that it does work. Then there is light, the greater light to rule the daytime of the novel, and the lesser light to rule the night scenes, breakfast and dinner, one day, and the gathering together of now this and now that group of characters to make a lively scene, grass, trees, apple trees in bloom, adequate provision for sea monsters if they turn up in a figure of speech, birds, cattle, and creeping things, and finally and especially man—male and female, Anna and Count Vronsky, Emma and Mr. Knightly.

There is not only all this, there are certain aesthetic effects that haven't been arrived at accidentally; the universe of the novel is beautiful, if it *is* beautiful, by virtue of the novelist's intention that it should be.

Say that the performance is successful; say that he has reached the place where an old, old woman, who was once strong and active and handsome, grows frail and weak, grows smaller and smaller, grows partly senile, and toward the end cannot get up out of bed and even refuses to go on feeding herself, and finally, well cared for, still in her own house with her own things around her, dies, and on a cold day in January the funeral service is read over her casket, and she is buried. . . . Then what? Well, perhaps the relatives, returning to the old home after the funeral, or going to the lawyer's office, for the reading of the will.

In dying, the old woman took something with her, and therefore the performance has, temporarily at least, come to a standstill. Partly out of fatigue, perhaps, partly out of uncertainty about what happens next, the novelist suddenly finds it impossible to believe in the illusions that have so completely held his attention up till now. Suddenly it won't do. It might work out for some other novel but not this one.

Defeated for the moment, unarmed, restless, he goes outdoors in his bathrobe, discovers that the morning is more beautiful than he had any idea—full spring, with the real apple trees just coming into bloom, and the sky the color of the blue that you find in the sky of the West Indies, and the neighbors' dogs enjoying themselves, and the neighbor's little boy having to be fished out of the brook, and the grass needing cutting—he goes outside thinking that a brief turn in the shrubbery will clear his mind and set him off on a new track. But it doesn't. He comes in poorer than before, and ready to give not only this morning's work but the whole thing up as a bad job, ill advised, too slight. The book that was going to live, to be read after he is dead and gone, will not even be written, let alone published. It was an illusion.

So it was. So it is. But fortunately we don't need to go into all that because, just as he was about to give up and go put his trousers on, he has thought of something. He has had another idea. It might even be more accurate to say another idea has him. Something so simple and brief that you might hear it from the person sitting next to you on a train; something that would take a paragraph to tell in a letter . . . Where is her diamond ring? What has happened to her furs? Mistrust and suspicion are followed by brutal disclosures. The disclosure of who kept after her until she changed her will, and then who, finding out about this, got her to make a new will, eight months before she died.

The letters back and forth between the relatives hint at undisclosed revelations, at things that cannot be put in a letter. But if they cannot be put in a letter, how else can they be disclosed safely? Not at all, perhaps. Perhaps they can never be disclosed. There is no reason to suspect the old woman's housekeeper. On the other hand, if it was not a member of the family who walked off with certain unspecified things without waiting to find out which of the rightful heirs wanted what, surely it could have been put in a letter. Unless, of course, the novelist does not yet know the answer himself. Eventually, of course, he is going to have to let the cat—this cat and all sorts of other cats—out of the bag. If he does not know, at this point, it means that a blessing has descended on him, and the characters have taken things in their own hands. From now on, he is out of it, a recorder simply of what happens, whose business is with the innocent as well as with the guilty. There are other pressures than greed. Jealousy alone can turn one sister against the other, and both against the man who is universally loved and admired, and who used, when they were little girls, to walk up and down with one of them on each of his size 12 shoes. Things that everybody knows but nobody has ever come right out and said will be said now. Ancient grievances will be aired. Everybody's character, including that of the dead woman, is going to suffer damage from too much handling. The terrible damaging facts of that earlier will must all come out. The family, as a family, is done for, done to death by what turns out in the end to be a surprisingly little amount of money, considering how much love was sacrificed to it. And their loss, if the novelist really is a novelist, will be our gain. For it turns out that this old woman—eighty-three she was, with a bad heart, dreadful blood pressure, a caricature of herself, alone and lonely—knew what would happen and didn't care; didn't try to stop it; saw that it had begun under her nose while she was still conscious; saw that she was the victim of the doctor who kept her alive long after her will to live had gone; saw the threads of will, of consciousness, slip through her fingers; let them go; gathered them in again; left instructions that she knew would not be followed; tried to make provisions when it was all but too late; and then delayed some more, while she remembered, in snatches, old deprivations, an unwise early marriage, the absence of children; and slept; and woke to remember more—this old woman, who woke on her last day cheerful, fully conscious, ready for whatever came (it turned out to be her sponge bath)—who was somehow a symbol (though this is better left unsaid), an example, an instance, a proof of something, and whose last words were—But I mustn't spoil the story for you.

At twelve o'clock, the novelist, looking green from fatigue (also from not having shaved), emerges from his narrative dream at last with something in his hand he wants somebody to listen to. His wife will have to stop what she is doing and think of a card, any card; or be sawed in half again and again until the act is letter-perfect. She alone knows when he is, and when he is not, writing like himself. This is an illusion, sustained by love, and this she also knows but keeps to herself. It would only upset him if he were told. If he has no wife, he may even go to bed that night without ever having shaved, brushed his teeth, or put his trousers on. And if he is invited out, he will destroy the dinner party by getting up and putting on his hat and coat at quarter of ten, causing the other guests to signal to one another, and the hostess to make a mental note never to ask him again. In any case, literary prestidigitation is tiring and requires lots of sleep.

And when the writer is in bed with the light out, he tosses. Far from dropping off to sleep and trusting to the fact that he did get home and into bed by ten o'clock after all, he thinks of something, and the light beside his bed goes on long enough for him to write down five words that may or may not mean a great deal to him in the morning. The light may go on and off several times before his steady breathing indicates that he is asleep. And while he is asleep he may dream—he may dream that he had a dream in which the whole meaning of what he is trying to do in the novel is brilliantly revealed to him. Just so the dog asleep on the hearthrug dreams; you can see, by the faint jerking movement of his four legs, that he is after a rabbit. The novelist's rabbit is the truth—about life, about human character, about himself and therefore by extension, it is to be hoped, about other people. He is convinced that this is all knowable, can be described, can be recorded, by a person sufficiently dedicated to describing and recording, can be caught in a net of narration. He is encouraged by the example of other writers—Turgenev, say, with his particular trick of spreading out his arms like a great bird and taking off, leaving the earth and soaring high above the final scenes; or D. H. Lawrence, with his marvelous ability to make people who are only words on a page actually reach out with their hands and love one another; or Virginia Woolf, with her delight in fireworks, in a pig's skull with a scarf wrapped around it; or E. M. Forster, with his fastidious preference for what a good many very nice people wish were not so.

But what, seriously, was accomplished by these writers or can the abstract dummy novelist I have been describing hope to accomplish? Not life, of course; not the real thing; not children and roses; but only a facsimile that is called literature. To achieve this facsimile the writer has, more or less, to renounce his birthright to reality, and few people have a better idea of what it is—of its rewards and satisfactions, or of what to do with a whole long day. What's in it for him? The hope of immortality? The chances are not good enough to interest a sensible person. Money? Well, money is not money any more. Fame? For the young, who are in danger always of being ignored, of being overlooked at the party, perhaps, but no one over the age of forty who is in his right mind would want to be famous. It would interfere with his work, with his family life. Why then should the successful manipulation of illusions be everything to a writer? Why does he bother to make up stories and novels? If you ask him, you will probably get any number of answers, none of them straightforward. You might as well ask a sailor why it is that he has chosen to spend his life at sea.

Contributors

Richard Bausch's novels include *Hello to the Cannibals, The Last Good Time,* and *In the Night Season.* His most recent book is *The Stories of Richard Bausch.* He is the recipient of a Lila Wallace–Reader's Digest Writer's Award and the Award in Literature from the American Academy of Arts and Letters.

Charles Baxter's most recent novels are *Saul and Patsy* and *The Feast of Love,* a finalist for the National Book Award. He has published four story collections and a book of essays about fiction, *Burning Down the House.* A recipient of the Award in Literature from the American Academy of Arts and Letters, he lives in Minneapolis and teaches at the University of Minnesota.

Benjamin Cheever has been a reporter for daily newspapers and an editor at *Reader's Digest.* He is the author of the acclaimed novels *The Plagarist, The Partisan,* and *Famous After Death;* a new novel is forthcoming in the summer of 2004. He has taught at Bennington College and the New School for Social Research.

Michael Collier's most recent book of poems, *The Ledge,* was a finalist for the National Book Critics Circle Award and the *Los Angeles Times* Book Prize. He is the director of the Bread Loaf Writers' Conference and teaches at the University of Maryland.

Annabel Davis-Goff's latest novel is *The Fox's Walk.* Her novels *The Dower House* and *This Cold Country* were *New York Times* Notable Books. She has also published a family memoir, *Walled Gardens.* She was born in the south of Ireland and lives in New York City.

Paula Fox's most recent book is the memoir *Borrowed Finery.* She has published five novels, including *Desperate Characters, The Widow's Children,* and *Poor George.* She is also a Newbery Award–winning children's book author. She lives in Brooklyn, New York.

Shirley Hazzard is the author of *The Transit of Venus,* winner of the 1981 National Book Critics Circle Award as well as *The Evening of the Holiday, The Bay of Noon,* and a memoir of Graham Greene, *Greene on Capri.* Her most recent novel, *The Great Fire,* won the 2003 National Book Award. She lives in New York City and Capri, Italy.

Anthony Hecht's seven books of poetry have been gathered together in *Collected Early Poems* (1990) and *Collected Later Poems* (2003). He is also the author of several volumes of criticism, among them *Melodies Unheard: Essays on the Mystery of Poetry* (2003). At eighty, he is one of America's foremost poets.

Edward Hirsch, a MacArthur Fellow, has published six books of poems, including *Lay Back the Darkness* (2003), and three prose collections, among them *How to Read a Poem and Fall in Love with Poetry* (1998), a national bestseller. He is president of the John Simon Guggenheim Memorial Foundation

Alice Munro has published ten collections of stories, including *Vintage Munro,* her most recent, and a novel, *Lives of Girls and Women.* She has received Canada's Governor General's Literary Award, the Lannan Literary Award, and the National Book Critics Circle Award, among other honors. She lives in Clinton, Ontario, and Comox, British Columbia.

Donna Tartt was born in Greenwood, Mississippi, and attended the University of Mississippi and Bennington College. She is the author of two novels, *The Secret History* and *The Little Friend,* and has published essays, poetry, and short stories in a number of magazines, including *Harper's* and *The New Yorker.*

John Updike, the author of more than fifty books, is an internationally known novelist, short-story writer, essayist, and poet. His novels have won the Pulitzer Prize (twice), the National Book Award, the National Book Critics Circle Award, and the Howells Medal.

Ellen Bryant Voigt has published six volumes of poetry, the most recent of which, *Shadow of Heaven,* was a finalist for the 2002 National Book Award, and a collection of essays, *The Flexible Lyric.* She has received a Guggenheim Fellowship and a Lila Wallace–Reader's Digest Writer's Award. She lives in Marshfield, Vermont.

Alec Wilkinson has written seven books, including *Big Sugar, A Violent Act, My Mentor,* and *Mr. Apology.* He has been a Guggenheim Fellow and has won a Lyndhurst Prize, a Pushcart Prize, and a Robert F. Kennedy Book Award. Since 1980, he has been a writer at *The New Yorker.*

Permissions

From *Ancestors* © 1971 by William Maxwell, reprinted with the permission of the Wylie Agency, Inc.

From *The Element of Lavishness* © 2001 by the Estate of William Maxwell, reprinted with the permission of the Wylie Agency, Inc.

From *So Long, See You Tomorrow* by William Maxwell, copyright © 1979 by William Maxwell. Used by permission of Alfred A. Knopf, a division of Random House, Inc.

"Stolen" by John Updike copyright © 2003 by John Updike. First published in *The New Yorker*.

"Mr. Maxwell" by Donna Tartt copyright © 2004 by Donna Tartt.

"Maxwell" by Alice Munro copyright © 2004 by Alice Munro.

"A Story in the Dark" by Paula Fox copyright © 2004 by Paula Fox.